TEENAGER

First published in October 2020

British Library Cataloguing in Publication Data
A catalogue record for this book is available
from the British Library.

ISBN 978 1 78521 724 1

Library of Congress catalog card no. 2020941691

Published by J H Haynes & Co. Ltd,
Sparkford, Yeovil, Somerset BA22 7JJ, UK
Tel: 01963 440635
Int. tel: +44 1963 440635
Website: www.haynes.com

Haynes North America Inc.
859 Lawrence Drive, Newbury Park,
California 91320, USA

Printed and bound in Malaysia

TEENAGER

ALL YOU NEED TO KNOW IN ONE CONCISE MANUAL

Andrew Bryant

Contents

A word of caution

It may appear somewhat nonsensical to start a book by highlighting its limitations, but it's important that as the reader (and most probably a parent) you are forewarned.

Your teen (or impending teen), is a complex creation, and as such each chapter of this book could easily justify a sizeable volume of its own. Indeed, there are many books out there that go into much greater detail on each subject; but any parent actively involved in the raising of their child will find it impossible to digest everything they would wish to know in an ideal world.

That's where I hope you will find this book to be useful, providing a readable, informative and, most importantly, *practical* guide to understanding and supporting your teen. It is not necessary to read the chapters in order; however, I believe there is value in exploring all of them at some point. Forewarned is forearmed!

Statistics and technical language have been kept to the minimum, but I have attempted to provide relevant data to justify any claims. Data is derived from reliable sources such as the ONS (Office of National Statistics), but as with most statistics, surveys have drawn on limited sample groups and as such won't necessarily reflect your home location or your teen. While the book is noticeably UK-centric (it not being possible to consider all countries), it is hoped all parents will be able to acknowledge the universal challenges and joy we experience in living alongside our teens.

As a parting observation before you embark further – you may read some things that concern or even shock you about young people. But remember, *you* made it out of the teenage years just fine!

Didn't you . . . ?

The stranger in your home

(aka the teenager)

The teenage years are often fraught for all involved, and the fact you have picked up this book implies you are probably asking yourself, 'Where did it all go wrong?'

The attentive, doting friend who shared your home for a dozen years has morphed into a reclusive, belligerent lodger who lives upstairs. So, who is that stranger in your house, and how do you ensure they don't remain an elephant in the upstairs room?

It might come as a surprise to learn the concept of the teenager is relatively

↑ 1960s: Hippies, Woodstock, drugs, free love, mods versus rockers, the contraceptive pill.

↓ 1970s: Disco, punk, comprehensive education, the three-day week.

↓ 1980s: Thatcherism, high unemployment, home computers, the AIDs epidemic.

↑ 1990s: The Poll Tax riots, the Back to Basics campaign of government, SATs tests for 14-year-olds and the birth of Labour's Third Way under Prime Minister Tony Blair.

modern. A number of academics claim the birth of the teenager came in the form of a 1945 *New York Times* article, 'A Teen-Age Bill of Rights'. This document of entitlement drafted by the Jewish Board of Guardians set out ten rights that each American teenager should be due. However, across the Atlantic another publication was already being enacted in the form of the Education Act 1944 for England and Wales. The Act, often referred to as the Butler Act, established a clear distinction between primary and secondary education and abolished fees for state-run secondary education. In one brief moment this Act not only increased our children's access to academic tuition but prolonged the period of *childness* to cover some of the teen years. And from that point on the growth of the teenager was relentless. From 1945's state-established youth work to the high employment, post-war optimism and good wages of the 1950s that heralded increased independence, the development of youth speak, rock and roll music and youth fashion. For the first time in history, young people were no longer simply mini versions of their parents!

And so the teenager's journey continued through the decades, all of which brought varying degrees of excitement, hope, fear and challenge.

Teenagers were given little time to establish their place in society before the next fad or wave of paranoia appeared on the horizon. Now consider the unparalleled predicament of the teenager during the noughties and the 2010s – globalisation, the Internet, social media, ease of access to illegal drugs and pornography, the breakdown of traditional family units, the rise in violent youth crime and cases of mental health issues, gender fluidity, growing concerns around climate emergencies and an ever-increasing emphasis on academic achievement.

All in all, we can probably agree it's been quite a journey for young people over a relatively short period. To paraphrase Neil Armstrong, that's one giant leap for a teenager!

⬇ The Internet has transformed the way teenagers engage with the world around them.

But wait! Let's not be hasty. Before we lay all the blame at the foot of modern society, take a look at the following quote:

[Young people] would always rather do noble deeds than useful ones: Their lives are regulated more by moral feeling than by reasoning – all their mistakes are in the direction of doing things excessively and vehemently. They overdo everything – they love too much, hate too much, and the same with everything else.

(Aristotle)

That's right – over 2,000 years ago adults were expressing the same concerns as the parents of today! Maybe the truth of the matter is that as parents we are not simply keen to forget our *own* teenage past, but we actively seek to deny it! G.K. Chesterton probably summed it up nicely when he wrote:

I believe what really happens in history is this: the old man is always wrong; and the young people are always wrong about what is wrong with him. The practical form it takes is this: that, while the old man may stand by some stupid custom, the young man always attacks it with some theory that turns out to be equally stupid.

⬇ Aristotles' opinion of young people in ancient Greece was no different to that held by many parents in the 21st century.

Chapter 1

Home life

Understanding the dynamics of your teen's friends' family units

Your teen is part of a generation called Generation Z. This includes everyone born between 1995 and 2015. They are also defined by the World Health Organization (WHO) as an adolescent. That is any person between the ages of ten and nineteen.

According to the Office for National Statistics there are approximately 5.15 million teenagers in the UK making up 7.85% of the total population. For each of these teens their home life plays a significant role in shaping life experiences. They are all affected to some extent by the people and places around them, and as a result no two teenagers are the same, nor are the families in which they live.

For many years media promoted the

⬇ Your teen may experience a diverse range of family units within their peer group.

family as a traditional nuclear family unit: a married mother and father with children. The term is relatively modern, first appearing in 1925, but in recent years society has witnessed a rapid change in what constitutes a family unit. One survey even claims there are as many as 35 different family units! The most common groupings are nuclear (two parents, either opposite sex or same sex, with a child/children, married or cohabiting), single parent, grandparent, step-family and extended family.

The change in family units and society's view of what constitutes a family has been linked to a number of changes in society.

↑ Marriage rates are almost half what they were in 1940.

- The decline of marriage and the greater acceptance of cohabiting couples and those choosing to have children out of wedlock. Marriage rates are almost half what they were in 1940.
- People choosing to marry are doing so at a later stage.
- Reduced social pressure to conform to a faith-based marriage. Religious marriages number half what they were in the 1990s.
- Divorce is often viewed as a very costly process.
- Women are experiencing greater independence. Whereas marriage historically offered financial security, women now have the ability to control their income, education, property and relationships.

How does this affect my teen?

Regardless of your own family unit, your teen will be spending time socially and academically with other young people experiencing a broad range of family units, value systems and norms which you may have experienced only via TV or newspapers. Most young people are very accepting of alternative lifestyles, but be prepared for your teen to raise questions. If this happens, do not be critical of their peers' family units and do not influence your teen to be critical or to agree with your personal views.

Your teen may experience a new family unit through circumstances such as bereavement or divorce. If this is the case, allow time for your child to adjust. Keep an open dialogue with them and be honest, even if you have to explain there are certain things you are unable to discuss at that point in time. Talk about how roles in the family may need to change. Be aware that children may view family units differently depending on their age and – most importantly – never lose sight of the purpose of family units being to offer love, security and support.

Boundaries

Ask almost any teacher what young people want and the thing you are certain to hear more than anything, is boundaries. Indeed, as strange as it may seem, even the most rebellious young person craves boundaries, often because these are absent in the home environment. What's more, despite their outward bravado, how many young people are truly confident moving into adolescence or adulthood without even the slightest sense of apprehension or fear?

Boundaries are simply rules. These will be nothing new to most teens as they are a central part of any classroom. Most teachers will focus on as few rules as possible and will word these in a positive way rather than having a list of activities headed 'YOU WILL NOT . . .'. However, boundaries can prove more problematic in the home environment as the dynamic is often different between a parent and child compared to a teacher and pupil. Further issues may arise as home boundaries can be constrained by a host of legal, moral and religious concerns.

Enforcing boundaries

Have you ever really thought about what a difficult and relentless role you have as a parent? At the risk of alienating a section of readers, consider the quintessential English game of cricket. The game is played in a large oval, and the primary

↑ Parenting can be a lot like cricket!

object is to hit a leather-coated ball towards the boundary markers. Eleven players will be fielding to retrieve the ball, making it relatively achievable to cover a large portion of the pitch. Now, imagine your pent-up teenager is batting and for most of the game the only fielders are you and maybe a partner or relative. The ball could be hit in any direction, with any amount of force. Sometimes there will be gentle taps directly towards you. Other times it might be a high ball that takes some time to reach you, or a low ball that is more difficult to stop. What's certain is that you will always be kept on your toes. That's every minute, of every day, of every year! Get the picture? Now before we carry on, give yourself a quick pat on the back for having made it this far. You're doing a great job!

Pushing boundaries is a natural part of growing up. That doesn't mean your teen should get away without any consequence for their actions, but you shouldn't be shocked to see your growing child testing out boundaries. Remember, most of the boundaries your teen pushes against will be removed when they become an adult – how they spend money, how they speak, where they are allowed to go, what time they can return home and who they are friends with. Your teen is simply craving independence, and for them it can't come soon enough. Your job is to get them to this privileged position within the correct timescale and without incident.

Top tips to consider when setting boundaries

1. Establish clear boundaries. Your teenager wants them – no matter how loudly they protest. These can change periodically but must be shared and understood. Don't expect your teen to pick up boundaries by osmosis!

2. Being flexible with some boundaries will mean your teen is more likely to abide by others as they realise you are considering their wishes.

3. If you need to write down rules, keep them to as few as possible and word them clearly and in a positive way. Clothes will only be washed if they are placed in the washing basket. No phones during mealtimes.

4. Share rules as a family wherever possible. No phones at mealtimes should apply to all members of the family.

5. Be consistent! There's no surer way for both parties to fail than to keep shifting boundaries. If they need to move, make sure it's for a good reason, that your teen knows the reason why they're moving, and whether it's a temporary or permanent change.

6. Don't sweat the small stuff! Bedroom-tidying should focus on not being a health and safety hazard. The teenage years are a war zone consisting of numerous battles. The important thing is to win the war. Wasting your resources on a few minor skirmishes is not worth it in the long run. Your teenager will thank you for it and so will your sanity!

7. Be clear and exact in your language. If you want your teen home by 10pm then say by 10pm. Not around 10pm. You may not realise it, but even the most agreeable teenagers have the debating skills of a barrister and will relish the opportunity to demonstrate them.

8. Discuss boundaries with your partner before imposing them so there is no confusion and a common goal.

9. Periodically check your boundaries. Are they still appropriate? Have a valid explanation as to why that is the boundary. If you don't have one, then maybe it's time you rethink if it is necessary.

10. Do you have an exit strategy? If you've used up all your oxygen and the room is full of heat and friction – seek an exit! It may be better for both parties to sleep on the issue and resume in the morning when tempers are less frayed.

⬇ Make rules clear for all members of the family and explain why you have made them.

This list is simply a starting point for setting and enforcing boundaries. Although it's hopefully a useful springboard, it ignores deeper issues that would require an academic tome to do it justice. Whose boundaries? Whose morals and standards? However, assuming you are already doing what you can, try to remember that sometimes teenagers just do really silly things. They are not robots, nor are they adults and, most importantly, their actions are probably not a reflection on you!

Money

One of the biggest causes of friction within adult relationships is money – either the lack of it, the inability to access it or how it is spent. This is not surprising given research has found the average cost of raising a child from birth to 18 is £75,436 for a couple and £102,627 for a single parent!

These figures will probably mean little to your teenager, however their concerns around money are largely the same as most adults – the lack of it, the inability to access it and how it is spent. It's easy as an adult to forget how we felt as a young person entering the teenage years – finally achieving a taste of independence but lacking the financial means to do the things of which we dreamt. So, what do we know about the financial habits of the average teenager?

According to research by OneFamily, we can see from the table below that the average weekly spend of young people increases with age.

Age	Weekly spend
13	£13
14	£17
15	£20
16	£24
17	£42
18	£58
19	£68

⬇ Many young people see no long-term benefit in saving.

↑ Make it clear what is paid for by you and what is paid for by your teen.

It will probably come as no surprise to you to find your teen's money is big business, contributing to £1.7 billion spent by young people each year in the UK. Of this, 84% is spent on clothes, socialising, food and gaming, with many young people declaring it is not worth saving as they will never be able to afford a house. However, before you think too disparagingly of today's youth, it is probably worth acknowledging the financial habits of adults. In the UK one in four adults has no savings.

Young people's attitudes towards money may have changed little since you were a teen, but the way in which young people process and accrue financial independence is changing constantly. Digital payments are increasing and predicted to rise to 90% by 2028, although one survey suggests 84% of British parents still give pocket money, an average of £2 a week for under-fives to £9.50 for those 15 and over, in notes and coins.

Although pocket money can prove a contentious issue for parents, few would question providing a level of financial independence can be a good foundation for the myriad of financial transactions involved as part of adult life. It is common for young people to be taken in by media reports of exceptional incomes (or perceived incomes) of a very small number of individuals, so it's important your teen develops a realistic and balanced view of money and learns to respect it from an early age.

Practical ways to help your teen develop a responsible attitude towards money

- Budget as a family. Keep a spreadsheet of all routine expenditure such as food, utility bills, mortgage/rent, council tax, clothes, travel costs, pets, TV subscriptions, holidays, recreation and clubs, phones, Christmas and birthday presents, school fees and music lessons. Explain how these are prioritised, eg a home could be repossessed if mortgage payments are missed. If you do not wish to disclose your real expenditure, you can always mock up a budget.
- Take your teen on the main weekly supermarket shop or get them to help with the online order so they can get a real picture of the cost of feeding a family.
- Discuss what is paid for by you as the parent and what is the responsibility of your teen.
- Encourage saving. Explain about bank accounts (savings and current accounts), credit and debit cards, interest rates and hire purchase.
- Explain about the dangers of loan sharks and doorstep lenders. Such practices are illegal in the UK.
- Discuss tax and NI on earnings. It will come as a shock for most teens to discover the difference between gross and net incomes.
- Look at an estate agent's window and a car dealership to see the price of an average house or car. You can find the average UK house price by going to http://landregistry.data.gov.uk/app/ukhpi
- Discuss average incomes (in 2019 this was £27.5k) and the average salary for different jobs. These are often much lower than young people expect.
- Encourage your teen to shop around for the best deal. Internet purchasing can be an impulsive process and doesn't allow the purchaser any time for consideration. Always look for added costs, such as postage and details of their returns policy. Beware of Internet sales techniques, such as countdown timers on the screen or claims of low stock levels.
- If goods are ordered from abroad there may be added delivery or tax costs and it may be difficult or impossible to return faulty items or claim a refund.

⬇ Take your teen on the weekly shop so they understand the cost of essentials.

⬆ Unlike traditional shopping, Internet shopping can result in additional costs, such as postage and packing.

■ Encourage your teen to explore used goods. These can be a fraction of the price of new goods and may still come with a guarantee.

⬇ Look at an estate agent's window to explore house prices for your local area.

■ Keep allowance or pocket money payments regular. Would you like your employer to pay you on a different day each month?

■ Don't give your teen access to your own bank details or your debit and credit cards.

■ Explore digital payment into your teen's bank account. This can encourage saving as the money is not immediately in their hands. A withdrawal limit can be set on the account and your teen will be prevented from falling into debt. Although bank cards are safer than cash as they are protected against theft and fraud, there is a downside in that it can be easier for your teen to spend as they won't see their money physically reducing when they tap against a terminal in a shop.

■ Above all, model good money management to your teen. Pay bills on time, budget and save when possible.

Part-time employment

A particularly effective way of learning financial skills is for your teen to secure part-time employment. Part-time jobs are win-win. As well as providing a good source of income for your teen, they also look good on a CV and will teach them useful skills for their adult life. In the UK there is clear legislation on the type of work that can be undertaken by teens and the hours they can work. In most areas of employment the youngest age a child can work part-time is 13. They are also barred from working during school hours and in certain locations such as factories and industrial sites. The legislation around employment of minors is far too long to detail here, but comprehensive and up to date guidance can be found at www.gov.uk/child-employment

It is worth noting a large number of young people have adopted an entrepreneurial approach to part-time employment as a result of opportunities afforded by the Internet. Perhaps the most prolific approach has been vlogging via services such as YouTube, which has brought vast revenues for some young people as the result of advertising being connected to their videos by social media companies.

⬇ A part-time job can be win-win for your teen.

Socialising, house parties

Socialising is an important part of human life. In fact, some sociologists believe we have used socialising as a defence mechanism to help us ever since we started foraging for food during the daytime.

We have clearly moved a long way since prehistoric times, but most humans still crave human interaction, whether for safety, companionship, to simply share gossip or to make us feel better. One study even found the simple act of shaking hands was enough to release oxytocin and dopamine, which increases levels of trust, lowers stress and even relieves pain. It should therefore come as no surprise, and should be positively encouraged, that your teen seeks a social network. As with most adults, teens will seek to socialise with a peer group of a comparable age and similar interests. However, the method of socialising can be different for males and females. Girls often prefer to meet face to face in order to share issues, whereas boys are more reluctant to open up to their peers and are more prone to harbouring emotions. While this is perfectly normal for boys, it can create or exacerbate mental health issues that may manifest in physical outbursts or withdrawal from social situations.

It is also important to recognise that across all age ranges there will be natural introverts and extroverts. While there is nothing wrong with either characteristic, it's worth noting that some research has shown social people enjoy a longer life expectancy and experience greater levels of mental and physical activity. What's

⬇ Girls are more likely to want to socialise in person compared to boys.

more, face-to-face encounters are an important learning experience and will equip your teen with skills they will find useful in their future careers. It helps your teen meet a range of people from different backgrounds and will help them build tolerance, sympathy, empathy and understanding – particularly useful skills if they are also seeking a romantic partner!

Although most parents encourage socialising, it is important to remember your teen is prevented from accessing many of the pubs, clubs and other meeting places readily available to adults. They may also lack the financial resources to access sports facilities or restaurants and many youth services have been reduced or scrapped by local councils. It is also important to acknowledge some young people do not wish to meet in an organised setting but would prefer to

⬆ **It's best to consider all implications before agreeing to a house party.**

socialise in parks or recreation grounds. This is not always the best scenario as it can make your teen more vulnerable and may expose them to the elements, particularly during dark and wet evenings.

A solution that may be raised by your teen is that of a house party. This can mean anything from an innocent get-together of a small number of close friends for a film and pizza to an open-invite rave. Indeed, the media has delighted in highlighting seemingly well-intentioned gatherings that have been advertised on social media and resulted in extensive damage and police intervention. If you are contemplating letting your teen hold a house party you should consider all the implications before you give your consent.

Issues to consider when contemplating a house party

- Agree a limit on the number of friends and ensure you know their names.
- Make sure all attendees are known to your teen and the event is not advertised on social media.
- You may be happy for your teen's friends to consume alcohol or smoke, but other parents may not. If smoking is allowed is this inside or outside? If allowed, then provide ashtrays in all locations. Remember, illegal drugs are *illegal*.
- If alcohol is allowed, consider providing the drinks and banning people from bringing their own. This way you can limit the intake. Do not serve spirits and ensure soft drinks and water are readily available (maybe including fruit punch or virgin cocktails). A number of teens will opt for these in preference to alcohol or will swap to them after an initial alcoholic drink.
- Provide snack food to prevent drinking on an empty stomach.
- Remove your own alcohol or lock it away.
- You have a duty of care to your teen's friends. As you will be *in loco parentis*, you will have to exercise the same care for other young people in your house as you do for your own – assuming you already exercise adequate care!
- Have at least one other adult present. Adults can always remain out of sight, but within earshot, in another room.
- Establish rules and boundaries before the event. Who will clean up? Are certain rooms out of bounds? What should happen if someone falls ill or drinks too much? Have emergency numbers been shared with your teen?
- Remove anything you don't want broken or stolen.
- Is it a sleepover? If so, where are people sleeping and will males be separated from females? If it isn't a sleepover, is there a curfew?
- Notify neighbours and let them know you will be present.

Many of these will still be valid questions if your teen is going to a house party. You may also wish to consider:

- Will it be held in one place or various locations? Where is it and is there a number you can call in case of emergency?
- How will they get there and back? Do they have money for a taxi? (Ensure your teen knows never to get into a car with someone under the influence of drink or drugs.)
- Do the host's parents know about the party?
- Does your teen have access to a mobile phone? Will they allow you to text to check they are OK?
- What is the latest time you expect them to be home?
- Your teen may be too embarrassed to leave a party early or to let you know something bad has happened. Agree a code word or phrase that can be used to let you know things are not going as planned or if they need to be picked up.
- Most importantly, as a parent you need to be reassured. If you don't receive adequate answers to your questions, then simply don't let them go. Explain why to your teen, prepare for tears and stick to your convictions.

Managing disagreements and defusing difficult situations

For most teens, as with adults, the downside to socialisation is the potential for disputes and disagreements. Your concern should not be *if* they happen, but how your teen is able to cope *when* they happen.

Dispute resolution is a real issue in the business world. The Thomas–Kilmann Conflict Mode Instrument is used by some companies to identify five different styles of conflict: competing, avoiding, accommodating, collaborating and compromising. These can also be applied to social and family settings. Which of these sounds closest to the method employed by you and your teen when conflicts arise?

1 **competing** is power-oriented and an individual pursues their concerns at another's expense.
2 **collaborating** involves working with another person to find a solution that satisfies the concerns of both parties.
3 **compromising** means finding a mutually acceptable solution that

↑ Conflict resolution can be employed within the family as well as in the workplace.

partially satisfies both parties and may involve concessions on both sides.
4 **avoiding** involves not immediately pursuing your concern, or someone else's, in order to avoid conflict.
5 **accommodating** involves neglecting your own concerns to satisfy the concerns of the other party.

Chances are you have tried one or more of these methods on a number of occasions and can probably spot the pros and cons of each. So, what approach should we adopt as parents?

■ Most importantly, try to avoid issues occurring in the first place. This may seem pointless when you're already facing a showdown with your teen, but how can you prevent this from happening again? What was the source or trigger point of the issue?
■ Listen! Don't expect your teen to listen to you if you haven't done them the

courtesy of listening to them. There are two sides to every story. That doesn't mean all stories are factual, but it's important for both sides to have an opportunity to express their concerns.

■ Explain why you feel the way you do. Try to use the word 'I' instead of 'you'. This is less accusatory and will help your teen to realise the impact their actions may have on others. Always use words and concepts your teen can understand.

■ Consider if there is some common ground you share or if you can compromise to suit both parties. Your teen may be willing to compromise if they realise the answer is not a simple 'no'. For example, 'you need to stay in tonight because of X, however I would be happy for you to go out tomorrow night', or, 'we need to eat a healthier meal tonight but how about we get take-away at the weekend?'

■ Try to remain calm and be aware of your body language. Avoid crossed or

⬆ Try to avoid mimicking your teen's gestures.

flailing arms, eye-rolling and finger-pointing. It's easier said than done, but your teen will often mirror your body language and tone of voice. This is an actual psychological trait of humans called limbic synchrony. Your teen will find it harder to react if they realise this is not simply a power struggle.

■ Realise that sometimes your teen may prolong a disagreement simply to test the boundaries. If you're adamant about your position, do not give the impression it will change. False hope will simply lead to further upset and resentment.

■ Be willing to admit when you are wrong. A little humility can go a long way!

It would be nice to think all disagreements can be solved by applying the above suggestions, but some parent–teen relationships reach a point where more significant intervention is required.

How to deal with the situation when a parent–teen relationship breaks down

It is important that both you and your teen feel able to call time on an argument. If the relationship hasn't reached a point where there is no chance of a resolution it may be beneficial to take time out or sleep on an issue. This can help tempers defuse and will allow both parties an opportunity to reassess their standpoint. However, if there appears to be no chance of resolution and the issue is critical you may have to mobilise an escape strategy.

- Contemplate alternative housing arrangements. Can your teen spend time with a relative or friend? Long-term housing provision may require the assistance of your local council.
- Consider mediation. Your teen's school will have access to counselling services, or you could explore provision such as Relate Counselling. You or your teen may also find it helpful to discuss issues with a friend or relative, but the third party should be neutral and removed from the issue or their views may not be respected.
- In extreme cases, where there is the threat of physical assault, do not be afraid to call for police support.

Under-18 housing

As a parent you cannot stop your teen leaving home by locking doors or physically restraining them. However, if your teen chooses to leave home and has reached what is known as the age of discretion (around 16), it is unlikely a court would force your teen to return home.

Your local council has a duty of care to young people that includes housing.

However, it is a myth to think a young person can demand council accommodation. Your council will attempt to keep your teen in the family home unless they are deemed to be in immediate danger. The legislation relating to young people's housing is complex, so anybody contemplating a change in their teen's housing provision should always consult an under-18s housing adviser via their local county council or unitary authority.

⬇ Counselling may be an appropriate route when relationships break down.

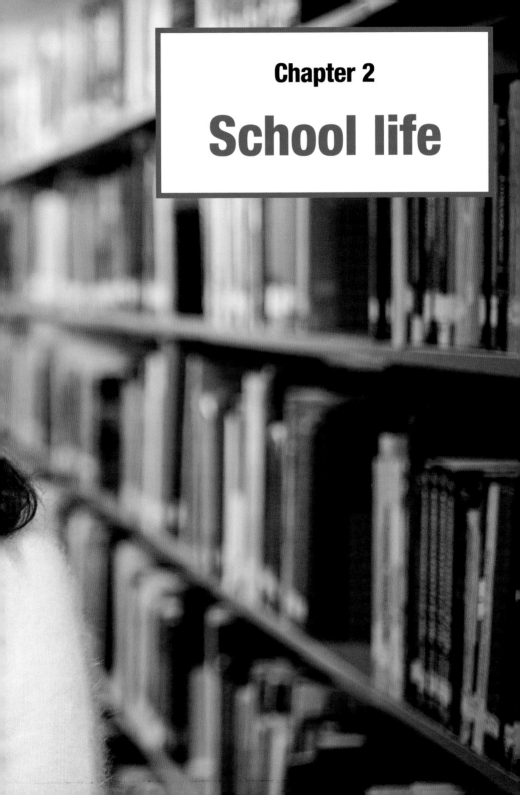

Chapter 2
School life

Bullying

A 2019 report found 20% of young people in the UK had been bullied in the previous 12 months. Of these, 75% claimed the bullying affected their mental health, a finding in accord with numerous sociological studies indicating persistent bullying can result in depression, anxiety, under-achievement, isolation and self-harm.

Although these figures will be of concern to both young people and parents, one reassuring statistic from a Department for Education survey shows levels of bullying fell with each year of increased age – from 22% of 10-year-olds to 8% of 15-year-olds. This decrease may be due to the way in which younger children perceive bullying and that older teens have developed greater resilience and emotional maturity.

Bullying can take many forms, including physical, verbal, social (mimicking, excluding, slandering and damaging reputations), cyber (via the Internet) and sexual. Just as bullying takes many forms, so do the bullies, who have different motivations and characteristics.

Bullying is an aspect of human interaction and will be evident in your teen's school regardless of teachers' claims. In fact, one question never to ask a school is 'do you have bullying?' Rather it should be, 'how do you deal with incidents of bullying?' That's not to say as parents we should be indifferent to bullying. Instead we should be equipping our teens with strategies to tackle it.

Schools are considered to be in loco parentis and as such they have a legal duty of care towards your teen. If you suspect your teen is being bullied, speak first with your teen and hear their side of

⬇ Cyber-bullying is on the rise.

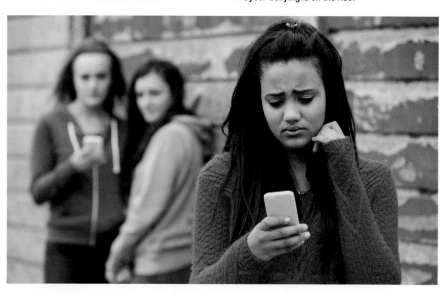

⬆ Bullying is inherent in all schools, regardless of what teachers may tell you!

Types of bullies

- **Bully victims** often bully others because *they* have been bullied. It is a way of reasserting themselves.
- **Popular bullies** feed off their followers to sustain their place in a pecking order.
- **Relational bullies** often dictate who is popular and who isn't (a common tool of girls).
- **Serial bullies** are systematic and manipulative in their approach.
- **Group bullies** often act in a different way when part of a group so as not to lose face.
- **Indifferent bullies** lack empathy and can display deep psychological issues.

the story. Never intervene directly with another young person. If you feel your teen has grounds for concern always approach a teacher or designated child welfare member of staff in the first instance. If you feel the incident has not been resolved adequately you can escalate the matter to a head of house/head of year, a senior manager, the headteacher and ultimately the chair of governors. Depending on the type of school it may also be possible to raise your concerns with the academy provider or the education department of your local authority.

Before approaching your teen's school it would be wise to be aware of the school's policy on bullying. This should be available on request and is often posted online on the school's website. You should also consider what it is you want to achieve and be realistic in your expectations. Always focus on *your* child, not on hearsay from the playground or other parents, and make sure you document responses from both your teen and the school. Ask what action will be taken, by whom and when, and as hard as it may be to accept, be prepared that the real story may not be so clear-cut. The bully may in fact turn out to be *your* teen! It happens more often than parents would like to acknowledge.

Never encourage your teen to retaliate. This may be an unpopular stance for some parents, but bullies rarely target people they believe are physically stronger than themselves. This not only places your teen at great physical harm but also risks *them* getting in trouble with the school or police. Your role is to teach your teen skills for life. Can you imagine the outcome if an adult chose to hit someone in the workplace to resolve a dispute?

It is also important to recognise your role in creating positive opportunities for your teen. Encourage them to leave valuables at home, ensure they leave for school with clean clothes, brushed teeth and the necessary books and resources and make sure they know a safe place to which they can go if any issues arise.

School policies and sanctions around bullying

Whether your teen is the bully or the bullied, their school should have in place a documented behaviour policy – including sanctions for poor behaviour. These should not exceed any stipulations laid down by government and can include a telling-off, a letter home, removal from a class or group, isolation, the confiscation of items and detention. The school doesn't require your consent to search if they believe your teen has prohibited items and are not required to give parents notice of after-school detentions or tell them why a detention has been given. School staff can use 'reasonable force' to control and restrain pupils. In extreme cases headteachers can exclude a pupil, even if an incident occurred outside the school.

Exclusions

If your teen is excluded the school will contact you to explain the reason for their decision and the length of exclusion. You will have the right to challenge this decision. It will be your responsibility to ensure your teen is not in a public place during school hours for the first five days of any exclusion. If this is not adhered to you will risk prosecution.

Exclusions can be fixed-period or permanent (meaning your teen is expelled). Fixed-period exclusions are temporary and for up to 45 school days in one school year. Schools should provide work for the first five days of an exclusion. Any period longer than five days should be catered for on a full-time basis by an organisation or institution arranged by the school.

Permanent exclusion, also known as expulsion, means your local council must arrange for your teen's education from the sixth school day after expulsion. Full details pertaining to exclusions can be viewed at www.gov.uk/school-discipline-exclusions/exclusions.

Managed moves

An alternative to permanent exclusion can be a managed move that allows your teen a fresh start at a new school. Managed moves require the consent of all parties, including your teen. As well as protecting your teen's school record they are regarded as financially beneficial to schools.

Home schooling

Although education is compulsory for young people in England, formal schooling is not. This is clearly defined in Section 7 of the Education Act 1996, which states:

The parent of every child of compulsory school age shall cause him to receive efficient full-time education suitable – (a) to his age, ability and aptitude, and (b) to any special educational needs he may have, either by regular attendance at school or otherwise.

Parents therefore have the right to choose to educate their children at home via what is termed as 'elective home education' or 'home schooling'. A House of Commons briefing paper published in July 2019 estimated that in 2018 up to 58,000 young people were home-educated in England. The reasons for home education are numerous and varied; however, common explanations relate to health/emotional health, religious or cultural beliefs and dissatisfaction with formal schooling.

While home education can offer many benefits (a tailor-made curriculum catering for interests and paced appropriately, relaxed working environments with

⬇ Parents have the right to home-school their children.

individual attention, no bullying or peer pressure, no compulsory homework or restrictions on hours or holidays) you should only choose to home educate your teen having considered carefully the full range of implications. These include:

⬆ Parents contemplating home schooling should consider carefully if they have access to required resources.

- ▩ Who will be teaching?
- ▩ Do I have time to commit to my teen's education on a regular basis?
- ▩ Where will my teen study?
- ▩ Will they have contact with their peer group?
- ▩ How will I assess my teen's progress and academic level?
- ▩ Will I have access to subject-specific equipment (particularly science and IT resources)?
- ▩ To whom can we turn if my teen needs targeted academic or pastoral support?
- ▩ Is there a home-schooling network that offers local support?
- ▩ Can I fund the resources and examination fees?
- ▩ Am I aware of how to access advice and guidance on careers and applying to further and higher education?

It is vital you first discuss your intentions with local parents of home-educated teens and visit home-education support groups where possible. Do not sign any release forms presented by your teen's school without receiving independent external guidance and being fully confident in your decision. A commitment to home school your teen should be made by you and your teen and should not be forced on you by your teen's school.

You will be responsible for informing the school if you wish to educate your teen at home. The school cannot refuse this request, although they can refuse to enter into a part-time education contract alongside home education. Be aware that if your teen is subject to a school attendance order, or if they attend a special school because of special educational needs (SEN), you will require your local authority's permission to home educate. Full guidelines on legislation around home education can be found on the government's website at gov.uk/home-education.

My teen doesn't 'fit in'

Almost all young people go through a stage of feeling they don't fit in. For some this will be short-term or periodic, though for others it may last their entire childhood and even into adulthood.

While most parents realise there is nothing wrong with being considered different from the crowd, and in fact this can be a virtue to be valued, it will be little comfort to your teen and may result in them missing out on new opportunities and experiences. What's more, a sense of isolation is also linked to a decline in both mental and physical well-being and in extreme cases has been linked to suicidal tendencies.

Belonging allows us to feel part of something bigger than ourselves and is recognised as part of Abraham Maslow's hierarchy of needs.

The need to fit in or belong to a group is more than just some childish rite of passage. It's actually a part of human life to which sociologists refer as an intrinsic motivation. There can be numerous reasons why your teen doesn't fit in – shyness, anxiety or a characteristic or limitation such as 'two left feet' in sport, or their voice, height, weight, self-conception of attractiveness or sexual orientation. Some teens will continue their path without adopting the characteristics of other young people, while others may choose to adapt their dress, affiliations and tastes to fit in with a peer group.

⬇ Maslow's hierarchy of needs.

Maslow's hierarchy of needs

- **Self-actualization** — desire to become the most that one can be
- **Esteem** — respect, self-esteem, status, recognition, strength, freedom
- **Love and belonging** — friendship, intimacy, family, sense of connection
- **Safety needs** — personal security, employment, resources, health, property
- **Physiological needs** — air, water, food, shelter, sleep, clothing, reproduction

↑ Not fitting in doesn't mean there is something wrong with your teen.

How can you support your teen?

■ **Listen!** Don't expect to understand the root of the issue if you don't allow your teen to explain themself. However, be aware explanations often hide the *real* concerns and sometimes these real concerns are not even recognised by your teen themself. No one is expecting

↓ Sorting out fact from fiction can sometimes seem an arduous task.

you to be a professional psycho-therapist, but try to discover your teen's *real concerns* in order to sift out fact from fiction. And don't assume that your teen is telling 100% of the story. Teenagers are apt to contort stories in their favour, just like many adults!

■ **Be sympathetic**, your teen is hurting, but also be empathetic where possible. Discuss your own past or present issues and how you have sought to resolve them. Explain that all humans lack confidence regardless of their outward persona. We live in an age where celebrity Instagram accounts portray an almost perfect existence. Your teen will often ignore the fact photos are frequently Photoshopped before being posted on celebrities' accounts, often not even by the celebrity themselves but by a PR firm, and teens may not be willing to accept they are being duped by their idols.

■ **Don't fight their battles for them.** Being concerned and empathetic is one thing, but wading into your teen's relationship issues is another. It won't help and will often make matters worse.

- **Build your teen's resilience** by giving them coping tools and creating meaningful opportunities. These may include role-playing so your teen can model responses, or signing up to a sports club or book group. Work from the starting point of what *they* would like to do. For the very anxious or introverted, an Internet forum could be a good place to build a friendship group; however, there are inherent dangers in that young people do not always know to whom they are talking and it isn't a long-term solution to facing real-world interactions.
- **Encourage your teen to have faith in their own convictions.** Don't try to mould them into someone they don't want to be. You are encouraging them to be confident in their own skin and with their own ideas – not someone else's. Spur them on to be a leader and not a follower. If no one chooses to follow, then they will be one of life's most revered – a true innovator.
- **Are there issues that can be addressed?** Is a new wardrobe or haircut in order? Can a weight issue be rectified by starting an exercise and healthy eating programme? Can your teen join a club or organisation to cultivate new friendships?
- **Work with your teen's positives.** Try not to dwell on negatives, but explore, value and hone the things at which they are good.

There is a lot of truth in the saying, 'you don't choose your friends, your friends choose you'. Your teen needs to recognise school friends are not always friends for life, and although they should be polite and approachable towards others, they are not required to be friends with everybody. Likewise, there is a difference between somebody not wanting to be a friend and somebody who is actively bullying.

We all make such choices on a regular basis. We often choose friends who are similar to us as it makes it easier to converse about our interests and strengthens what sociologists refer to as plausibility structures – the physical or social frameworks that reinforce our belief that we are making wise choices.

That's not to say schools can't be brutal environments (if a similar level of bullying happened in the workplace the perpetrators would be reprimanded or fired) and for some young people there is no easy answer. This is not your failing as a parent. The ability to make progress will depend largely on the emotional maturity of your teen. If issues persist it may be useful to seek the support of professional counselling, particularly if there is the threat or evidence of self-harming.

⬇ A resilient teen should be the wish of every parent.

Special educational needs, dyslexia, autistic spectrum disorder

This book is not a medical journal and in no way seeks to replace guidance from a GP or other health professional. However, it would be a disservice not to acknowledge the rise in awareness and diagnosis of certain conditions affecting young people.

Dyslexia

Dyslexia is a common learning difficulty that can cause problems with reading, writing and spelling. It is estimated that at least 10% of the population is dyslexic, accounting for approximately 870,000 children in England. However, it is feared schools are failing to diagnose at least 80% of dyslexic pupils and 95% of parents

◆ Dyslexia can often obscure the true ability of a young person.

feel they lack skills and knowledge to support their dyslexic child.

Although a diagnosis should always be sought from a professional trained in dyslexia, common symptoms of dyslexia include:

- Repeatedly rereading texts in order to comprehend.
- Difficulty with handwriting, spelling, word and letter order, written explanations, maths equations,

deadlines, note taking, processing information and formulating more complex sentences.

- A significant discrepancy between your teen's school performance and scores on standardised tests.

Be aware your teen may be embarrassed by these symptoms and will try to hide them from you or their teachers. It may also be the case that your teen is suffering the effect of a different ailment, such as a hearing or vision problem, so it would be wise to rule these out as part of the assessment process.

If you have any concerns, discuss these with your teen's school in the first instance. Many schools will have a trained dyslexia teacher or assessor. If you are not happy with their evaluation you will still be able to consult a GP or private assessment clinic.

If deemed necessary, a pupil-specific plan can be implemented by the school. Pupils needing a higher level of support may be provided with an education, health and care plan (EHCP).

ASD/ASC

Autistic spectrum disorder (ASD) and autistic spectrum condition (ASC) are terms that cover autism, Asperger's syndrome and pervasive developmental disorders. Autism is not a disease or illness and neither does it have a cure. People with autism are born that way or display symptoms from a young age.

Asperger's describes people with autism but with average or above average intelligence. This is sometimes referred to as high functioning autism and is no longer something diagnosed by medical professionals.

Symptoms of ASD/ASC will vary from teen to teen both in type and severity; however, common symptoms include difficulty in making friends, understanding and expressing feelings, inference and idioms and changes to routines. Sufferers of ASD/ASC also often have a keen interest in certain subjects, items or activities.

ADHD

Attention deficit hyperactivity disorder (ADHD) is concerned with inattentiveness, hyperactivity and impulsiveness. Most, but not all ADHD sufferers have issues with all these traits and their condition will be noticeable by the age of six. Those suffering inattentiveness issues are classed as having attention deficit disorder (ADD) and can sometimes be misdiagnosed by parents or teachers as simply being lazy or uncooperative.

Common symptoms of inattentiveness include a short attention span, making careless mistakes and difficulty prioritising tasks. Common symptoms of hyperactivity and impulsiveness include constant fidgeting and talking, interrupting speakers and a poor awareness of risk.

These symptoms can be a significant source of unease for your teen and can lead to academic underachievement, anxiety and difficulties with relationships and securing employment. However, for many young people the symptoms of ADHD lessen or disappear as they grow older.

Treatment will vary depending upon the needs of the individual, however this could include one or more of a variety of medicines licensed for use in a particular country and/or counselling such as cognitive behavioural therapy, psychotherapy or family therapy.

Dyspraxia

Developmental coordination disorder (DCD), also known as dyspraxia, is the result of developmental issues relating to the part of the brain concerned with physical coordination. Your teen would struggle to meet age-appropriate tasks and may appear to move in a clumsy fashion. This can be particularly evident during sporting activities such as kicking, catching and throwing. It can affect both sexes, but most cases involve males.

Although the exact cause of dyspraxia is unknown, some factors may include premature birth, family history of DCD or the consumption of alcohol or drugs during pregnancy. There is no cure for DCD, but schools should be able to adapt tasks to make learning and movement easier for your teen by arranging furniture and seating, breaking activities down into smaller tasks and providing dedicated resources such as grips for pens and pencils, touchscreens and dictation software. Treatment for DCD varies from individual to individual, but usually involves occupational therapy to develop fine and gross motor skills.

ODD (oppositional defiant disorder) and CD (conduct disorder)

While all young people have periods of poor behaviour, if your teen demonstrates extreme behaviour issues for at least six months they may be suffering from oppositional defiant disorder (ODD).

Symptoms will regularly hamper their ability to engage in their education or relationships, both socially and at home, and will often include frequent temper issues, irritability, excessive arguing, refusal to abide by rules, vindictiveness and vengefulness.

Diagnosis is made employing a checklist of symptoms, exploring the frequency and timescale of behaviour, and treatment is usually via behavioural therapy and/or medication. The role of the parent is central to the treatment of ODD and therapy may include joint sessions involving both parent and teen.

Conduct disorder (CD) is a more acute form of ODD and may include severe aggression, cruelty to people and animals, theft, arson, vandalism and truancy. As with ODD, treatment is usually via behavioural therapy and/or medication.

I think my teen may have an undiagnosed condition

If you are concerned about your teen it is important to discuss your concerns with your school's SENCO (special educational needs coordinator) who will be responsible for overseeing support and guidance for all young people with educational needs and EHCPs. There may be a number of reasons why your teen is not performing to the level you expect that have little or nothing at all to do with medical issues. A SENCO will discuss your teen with their tutor(s) and observe them in the classroom. They may also arrange for tests to be carried out to evaluate cognitive understanding or literacy levels. Although it is important not to compare your child with other children in their class, it may be informative and useful to understand where they rank in comparison to an average learner of that age. The SENCO may be able to arrange for certain evaluative tests to be carried out by the school. However, medical assessments would generally be undertaken by medical health professionals such as a GP or occupational therapist.

Homework

Love it or hate it, approve of it or think it should go the way of the dinosaurs, homework is probably a regular feature of your teen's daily activities. Given the correct level of attention it can be an important tool for consolidating learning received in school, and as such parents should do what they can to foster a productive attitude.

Perhaps of primary importance is that teenagers are entitled to a quiet space to complete their work. If at home this should be in a clean, quiet and safe environment at a suitable temperature and with adequate Internet access. If these features are not available at home, your teen should be able to access an appropriate space in their school, possibly as part of a designated homework club. Local libraries

⬇ Take an interest in your teen's homework but be careful not to complete it for them!

may also offer study rooms and even tutoring services.

It's not always appropriate for your teen to get straight down to homework after a day at school, but night-time homework sessions should be discouraged as few people are able to do their best work at a late hour, especially if sleep deprived. Your teen may find a homework plan of help in tackling procrastination, prioritising tasks and aiding exam revision. As a parent you may also find it useful to ban TV, phones and other distractions until homework is

completed. However, if homework is carried out over a lengthy period be aware of the need for your teen to programme adequate breaks. (You may even be the one who has to encourage this.)

Take an interest in your teen's homework. They are more likely to put greater time and effort into it if they think you are taking an interest and will be reviewing the finished work. Ask questions about the task, rather than just saying, 'do you have any homework?'.

Make sure your teen understands the task; but don't question them in detail – it's not an inquisition! And remember, the homework is to test them and assess *them*, not you! Don't fall into the trap of doing everything for them. It's OK to share your knowledge, but your main aim should be to hone their research skills and independent learning. Don't panic if your teen doesn't understand a concept or

⬆ Homework should not affect your teen's health and well-being. Know when to stop.

question. In the age of the Internet you can be sure that if you don't have the answer, someone in the world will and is only a mouse-click away.

Stay informed of allocated homework. A schedule is usually available for parents to access online. Don't rely on your teen to tell you anything! If you find your teen is receiving excessive homework on certain nights, it may be useful to speak to the school to see if the workload can be spread more evenly throughout the week. If homework takes beyond the allocated or suggested time, then explore why. If it is too easy or beyond the current scope of your teen, this should be discussed with the school. The purpose of homework is not to cause undue anxiety. Know when to stop!

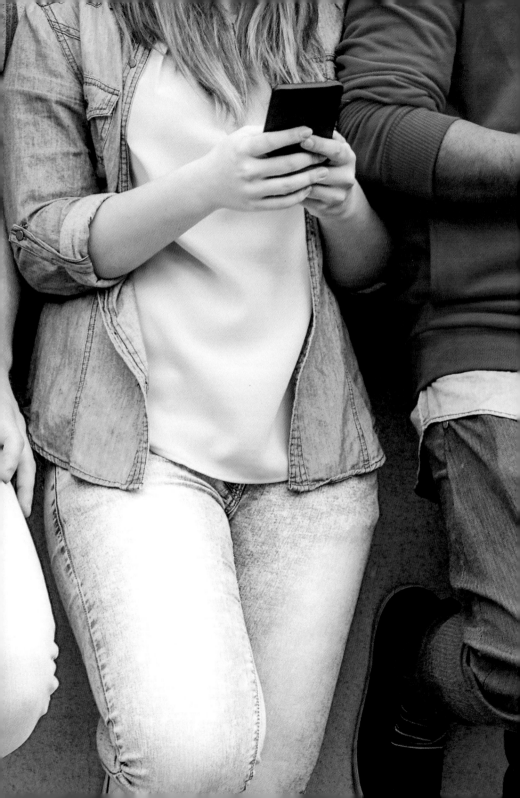

Chapter 3

Teen culture

Growing up earlier (or too soon)

Despite the extension to 'childness' referenced in the introduction to this book, in many ways young people are now viewed as growing up earlier. This probably comes as little surprise to most parents given the open-door nature of the Internet and proliferation of social media and viewing platforms.

Take the pervasive spectre of pornography as an example. Whereas for most parents of teens access to pornography was via a top-shelf magazine, young people now have every conceivable form of pornography beamed directly to their phone in the privacy of their own bedroom. It is much the same for risqué content on TV. A 9pm watershed still exists in the UK and there are limits as to what can be broadcast after that time, but it has little impact on the viewing habits of the average teenager when the majority are using platforms such as YouTube for their video content.

Emotional maturity/physical maturity

One of the frustrating aspects of teenage years, for parents and teens alike, is an expectation that emotional maturity will develop in line with physical maturity. Whereas your teen has little control over the changes happening to them physically, emotional maturity can be a more complex and traumatic journey. Emotional maturity encompasses aspects of behaviours and

⬇ The 9pm watershed has little impact in the age of the Internet.

attitudes and the ability of your teen to respond appropriately to challenging situations, employing qualities such as empathy, sympathy, self-worth and emotional control.

While physical maturity occurs around the age of 18, emotional maturity can take much longer to achieve. Some researchers found that although cognitive abilities mature by the age of 16, emotional maturity isn't reached until after the age of 22. The result (and it's not a positive one for parents) is a teen prone to potent emotional reactions and zealous obsessions that may seem irrational to the average adult.

If that's not confusing enough, emotional maturity may actually be linked directly to physical maturity. At least, that is, in relation to the physical maturity of the brain. Hold on to your hat – here comes the science part!

The teenage brain

Two areas within the brain experience rapid growth during the teen years – the

↑ The teenage brain. Best to think of it as a fine wine!

amygdala and the prefrontal cortex. In fact the brain continues to mature until the mid- to late 20s. (Think of it as a fine wine or cheese and it may make the whole teen experience more palatable!) The amygdala is concerned with emotions and motivation, while the prefrontal cortex, one of the last parts of the brain to mature, is concerned with a number of characteristics known as executive functions. These relate to self-control, focusing attention, planning, prioritising, problem solving and decision making.

Be aware that developmental rates for the amygdala and prefrontal cortex will vary from teen to teen. So when, not *if*, you reach those points of sheer bewilderment as to your teen's behaviour, attempt to remain calm, model good behaviour, and try to think of the teenage years as a medical condition for which the only cure is time!

Social networking apps

If there is one thing vying to be representative of teenage culture in the modern age, then social networking apps would be a prime contender. However, it's important as parents to realise that social networking in the broadest sense is nothing new. As humans we naturally seek to establish social networks and have always employed the resources of the day to assist us, whether that's printed media, TV or computers.

Social networking in today's terms refers principally to the range of apps and sites that allow us to connect with friends, family, retailers and people with similar interests or concerns via phones and computers. They are not only for young people; the business sector revolves around apps such as LinkedIn in order to promote their wares and attract suitable employees.

Given the increasing access to, affordability and speed of technology, social networking use has grown at an astonishing rate. According to one 2018 study:

■ 85% of 13–17-year-olds said they used YouTube, a site with 2 billion users where viewers can upload videos on any subject.
■ 72% used Instagram, a photo- and video-sharing site with 1 billion users.
■ 69% (190 million) used Snapchat, a photo- and message-sharing app where the sender of an image can limit the time the receiver can view the photo between 1 and 60 seconds.

⬇ Social networking apps have opened up the world to your teen.

However, all these apps pale in comparison to Facebook, the world's largest social network with almost 2.5 billion monthly active users.

Social networking is big business. While apps are usually free to download and use, they accrue most of their income via advertising. As a result, it is now rare to find any video or article online without at least one advert or celebrity endorsement. And advertisers have become increasingly inventive in finding ways of taking your teen's money. One recent and highly controversial method is known as sadfishing, whereby celebrities share supposed tales of woe in order to seek exposure and promote merchandise. However, it's not all a one-way transaction. The Internet, and particularly apps such as YouTube, have allowed anyone of any age to make money. In fact, in 2019 the highest paid 'influencer' on

⬇ Vlogging (video blogging) is not simply a hobby, it can be a business opportunity for your teen.

YouTube was a 7-year-old reviewer of toys, with an income of $22 million!

Parents are often concerned by the power and influence of social networking companies; however, these are high-profile organisations and as such are monitored closely by the relevant authorities and subject to numerous moral, ethical and financial constraints.

Of greater concern is the unregulated area of the Internet that most parents don't see or experience, known as the dark web.

The dark web

It is important to note that the dark web (also referred to as the darknet) is different to the deep web, which combined make up over 90% of the Internet. The deep web is full of private information such as your personal email accounts, passwords, medical records and banking details. These are legitimate and important files that can't be accessed by search engines because the information is confidential and

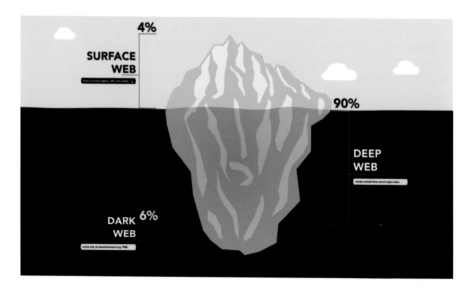

4%

SURFACE
WEB

90%

DEEP
WEB

DARK 6%
WEB

⬆ The dark web accounts for over 90% of the Internet.

highly regulated. However, the dark web is a very different and potentially more dangerous system.

To access the dark web your teen will require a special browser. There are several, such as Psiphon, I2P and Freenet, but the most popular is Tor. Tor stands for 'The Onion Router', and sites hosted by Tor all use a '.onion' suffix instead of the usual '.co.uk', '.com' or '.org'. It has three layers of encryption and is actually part-funded by the US government. Searches are not made by Google or Internet Explorer but via a dedicated dark web search engine. Popular search engines include DuckDuckGo, Onion URL Repository, Torch and notEvil.

By simply using TOR or other dark web software your teen is not breaking any law and many young people use the dark web simply to keep up with their peers, appear tech-savvy or to protect their identity. However, given the dark web's high level of anonymity it also provides a cover for a significant number of illegal activities. These include extortion, money laundering, extreme (illegal) pornography, sexual grooming, trading confidential information, slavery and the sale of illegal firearms and drugs. Even the currency used in many of the transactions on the dark web can be impossible to trace and recover as it

⬅ The Silk Road was perhaps the most notorious site on the dark web.

employs bitcoin, a digital currency independent of a central bank.

Perhaps the most notorious site on the dark web was Silk Road, which acted as a marketplace for illegal drugs. Advocates of the site claimed it provided a valuable service as it was safer for users to purchase drugs from the security of their home than to meet face to face with dealers on the street. Another highly popular site is 123Movies (which also trades under a number of similar names); a movie-streaming site which at its peak boasted 98 million users a month. However, the proliferation of such activities does not mean authorities are oblivious to what goes on within the dark web. Police and security forces both in the UK and abroad monitor the dark web on a continuous basis, so if your teen chooses to access it, they should consider some key tips in order to stay safe:

- ■ As with conventional Internet use, it is often not possible to know with whom you are communicating. Never give out personal information, especially your address, telephone number and bank details and do not log in to any accounts while active within the dark web.
- ■ Although accessing the dark web is not against the law, many activities that take place on there do break the laws of many countries. Dark web search engines do not monitor or rank the validity of sites they return. It can therefore be difficult to differentiate between legal and illegal sites and those attempting to scam and extort money.
- ■ Although your teen may claim that simply accessing some sites such as 123Movies is not illegal, the content signposted by the site may be illegal

and by streaming or downloading content they may be breaking the law and liable to prosecution.

- ■ Financial transactions carried out via the dark web are usually untraceable meaning it can be impossible to receive a refund for scam transactions or faulty goods. This is particularly the case when using bitcoin.
- ■ Always use a VPN (virtual private network). A VPN hides your computer's IP address and makes you anonymous to sites you visit.
- ■ Ensure your computer is running updated and reputable security software. Some experts also recommend covering your computer's camera and microphone with a piece of black tape. It may seem a bit extreme, but this is exactly what Mark Zuckerberg (co-founder of Facebook) famously does!

Finally, onerous as it may be, as a parent you should attempt to stay aware of changes in trends even if you are not using these apps yourself.

⬇ Some people attempt to enhance online security by covering their computer lens with tape.

Consequences of unregulated adult content accessed by teens

Given the nature of some of the unregulated content on the Internet, and the average teen's ability to evade age restrictions on websites and apps, it is not so much a case of *will* my teen view inappropriate content on the web, but are

↑ It is inevitable your teen will see something inappropriate on the Internet.

they equipped to cope with it *when* they view it.

The good news is that most of the extreme and illegal content on the web (especially sexual content involving children or animals) is more difficult to access than the media would have us imagine and can generally only be reached from within the dark web. That is not to say that a vast amount of graphic sexual content, sometimes even played out in real time, can't be found via a simple Google search or that content won't simply be passed to your teen by his or her peer group.

Pornography is a primary concern of most parents as it is no longer an issue of two-dimensional bodies in magazines, but close-up, high definition video catering for

← Pornography is no longer restricted to top-shelf magazines.

every taste and fetish imaginable. It is also often free of charge and can be streamed in the comfort of your teen's bedroom direct to their computer or mobile phone.

While a teenage interest in sex and the human body is a perfectly natural aspect of maturing into adulthood, some teens will be less equipped emotionally to assess what they are viewing. Many critics of Internet porn say the sex is often portrayed as an act removed from the safety and loving context of a relationship. They also have concerns over the level of violence and fetishes that become normalised and may place teens, particularly girls, under pressure to copy what they see on the Internet in order to please their partner.

The risks to your teen extend beyond pornography. Both males and females are bombarded with health-related content on a daily basis and there seems to be a relentless stream of new health crazes leading young people, teens in particular, towards a number of obsessive or addictive behaviours. In fact, the significant rise in hospital admissions over the past decade for potentially life-threatening eating disorders has been linked by many critics to the enormity of social media content, especially that portraying celebrity lifestyles. However, it's not all negative news. One 2018 study found 43% of young people believed health-related content on social media impacted positively on their health.

⬇ Filtering software is not 100% effective and can sometimes block legitimate sites.

How to protect your teen from inappropriate online content

■ The easiest solution, although not necessarily the best, is to install filtering software on all computers and mobile phones. The decision is yours, but be aware such software is not foolproof and some will attempt to block legitimate content (although you can unblock these websites if required). More importantly, you need to ask yourself how *you* would feel if you were subjected to a periodic review of your browser search history. Even if you had never visited a 'disreputable' site, you would probably feel mired in mistrust and doubt.

↓ Spying on your teen will undoubtedly be regarded as a major breach of trust.

■ Talk to your teen! Explain clearly and calmly what is expected of them and why you have made these rules. It should be acceptable for you as the parent to request that no explicit material is viewed in the house, especially if younger siblings are present.

■ Don't spy on your teen without very good cause. Beyond being viewed as a breach of trust, any teen attempting to access material they wouldn't wish their parent to see will be tech-savvy enough to cover their trail using incognito windows or a VPN connection.

■ Don't attempt to force a confession from your teen. If they are not prepared to give an answer, then you will probably end up with a lie.

- If you do find inappropriate material or search histories, remain calm when broaching the subject with your teen. They will probably be exceptionally uncomfortable and, unless the material is illegal or extreme, there is probably little value in discussing it at length.
- When claims are made about medicines or health regimes, don't make blanket remarks and expect your teen to believe you or to ignore the advertising. Take time to discuss the content and their intentions. Ask pertinent questions such as whether research was carried out by medical professionals rather than slating an idea because it's the latest fad with a celebrity your teen idolises on social media.
- Never open or respond to spam email and only download content from official sites.
- If your teen doesn't understand the context of content they have viewed, take time to discuss this with them or to research if you lack the knowledge yourself. Don't leave them to dwell on content they find uncomfortable or troubling. If the content came from your teen's peer group it may be appropriate to contact the safeguarding officer in your teen's school.
- Consider moving computers to a family room. However, this may prove inconvenient and disruptive, especially if your teen requires a quiet space for homework. It is also not such a workable solution given that these days all Internet content can be accessed via a mobile phone.
- Ensure passwords or pin codes are set up on media streaming devices such as Netflix in order to limit access to

⬆ Asking for IT support from your teen can open up conversation about online safety.

inappropriate content and that codes are not shared with your teen.
- Encourage your teen to create strong passwords and never share these with anyone, including siblings.
- Ask your teen for help with how you can protect *yourself* online. You will probably find they are a lot better informed than you imagine and their responses can open the door for a less confrontational conversation.
- Ensure social media profiles are set to private. Teens are often oblivious to the fact they leave a digital footprint with every click of the computer and this can come back to haunt them when applying for employment or university study.
- Remember, don't expect a 9pm watershed on the Internet like on terrestrial TV in the UK. Internet content is available 24/7. The only guaranteed solution is to remove your teen's mobile phone and computer from their room.

Gaming

It will come as no surprise to any parent of a teen to learn that video gaming is big business. The UK games industry employs over 47,000 people and, according to a 2018 report commissioned by the British Film Institute, the UK is the fifth largest video game market in the world with £5.11 billion spent on gaming in the previous year.

What may surprise some parents is that an increasing number of games are now free to download and play, with companies raising revenue through a mixture of advertising and in-game purchases. These purchases are often software-based game enhancements that boost a player's position or power in a game or reveal hidden features and levels. Many games also spawn gaming communities – a group of like-minded gamers who gather online to discuss features and tactics. These are generally safe communities, but as with all Internet activity your teen needs to ensure they never reveal their real name, location or any details about their school or banking details.

Although parents come under a lot of pressure to fund their teen's gaming interests, you should never link your credit or debit card details to your teen's gaming accounts. Any banking information required should be entered afresh with each transaction and only via webpages using secure transactions. The address for secure websites will begin with https://, the 's' standing for secure.

If you find your teen has accrued an unauthorised spend using your bank details, it may be possible to seek a refund by logging the incident with your card handler as 'friendly fraud'. This will be a matter between you and your bank, and the police will not be involved unless there was an element of coercion or fraud against your teen.

⬇ The UK gaming industry is worth over £5 billion per year.

Online safety

Despite numerous advancements the Internet has provided, it has also helped facilitate a growing list of evils, including sexting, revenge porn, grooming, radicalisation, cyber-bullying, fraud and identity theft.

SEXTING

Sexting (also known as trading nudes, dirties or pic for pic) refers to the sending and receiving of sexual images of yourself or others by a digital device.

Young people sext for the same reasons as adults: to flirt, to boost self-image, through peer pressure or as a form of revenge porn. However, while sexting is not illegal for adults, it is illegal to share explicit images of a child, even if the person sending the image is a child. A young person is committing a crime if they:

- take an explicit photo or video of themselves or a friend
- share an explicit image or video of a child, even if it's shared between children of the same age
- possess, download or store an explicit image or video of a child, even if the child gave their permission for it to be created.

Although your teen may protest that sexting is harmless, it can lead to a host of negative outcomes including bullying, extortion and mental health issues – not to mention the fact that images, over which they will no longer have control, will remain as a digital footprint for the rest of their life. Your teen should also be aware indecent images are not simply naked photos; they may be interpreted as indecent if they include sexualised poses in underwear or even a swimming costume.

- Save the evidence and take screenshots of web pages if required. Ensure these are stored using password protection and you do not forward them unless instructed by the police.
- Contact your local police force, either in person or by calling 101 in the UK.
- If images have been shared by an individual or group within your teen's school, speak with the school's designated safeguarding lead. Schools have the authority to search pupils' electronic devices and delete indecent images.
- If images have been uploaded to websites or social media platforms you may be able to request they are removed. This should only be requested in agreement with the police.
- Explain to your teen about the steps required. This will be embarrassing for most teens and they may try to convince you not to get involved.
- You can seek counselling for your teen through the school's designated safeguarding lead. Counselling can sometimes be arranged outside the school premises.
- Although you may be angry or disappointed, try to remain calm. Your teen will be the one suffering most embarrassment. If you wish to understand the level of distress they are feeling, imagine taking a naked photo of yourself, sharing it with your work colleagues, and knowing they have possibly shared it with total strangers on the Internet.

⬇ Revenge porn can be impossible to remove from the Internet.

REVENGE PORN

While sexting can appear perfectly innocent to some teens, a much more distressing aspect of sexting is when it is used as revenge porn. Revenge porn is the sharing of explicit images without the subject's consent and has become such a concern that in the UK there is now specific legislation against it. It is an offence under Section 33 of the Criminal Justice and Courts Act 2015 to disclose 'private sexual photographs or films without the consent of an individual who appears in them and with intent to cause that individual distress'. This applies to both online and offline images and covers any images considered to be sexual, whether showing an individual or group

'engaged in sexual behaviour or posing in a sexually provocative way'.

GROOMING

Grooming refers to the practice of communicating with a child for the purpose of abusing them. This includes facilitating somebody else's actions or performing a sexual act in the presence of a minor. A conviction for grooming can incur a prison sentence of up to 14 years.

While grooming is not new, the ease and anonymity afforded by the Internet has led to a rapid growth in cases of online grooming. According to findings by the NSPCC in 2019, 5,161 crimes of sexual communication with a child were recorded in England and Wales over a period of 18

⬆ **Vulnerable teenagers often do not realise they are being groomed.**

months and there was a 200% rise in the use of Instagram to target children.

Although it is important for parents to recognise the signs of grooming, it is just as vital your teen recognises them. Be aware many children do not know, or are not willing to accept, they are being groomed. Individuals and groups grooming children are often very subtle and convincing when approaching young people and will prey on their insecurities.

Although almost all schools will discuss grooming as part of their curriculum, it is important your teen is aware of your concern and you are both mindful of the potential dangers. Common signs of grooming include:

- Your teen sending a large amount of text messages and hiding conversations from you.
- Sexualised requests or intimate questions about partners and sexual experiences.
- Your teen changing friendship groups or meeting friends in new and possibly less-public locations.
- A reluctance to discuss new friends or to bring them to the family home.
- Requests to your teen for personal information and being asked to keep or share secrets.
- Being asked to move into a private chatroom online or to DM (direct message).
- Being asked to meet up but not to tell anyone.
- The appearance of a second mobile phone.
- Your teen using a VPN or incognito

⬇ The use of a VPN can be a sign of responsible Internet use. However, it could also indicate something more sinister.

windows in order to hide Internet use or closing browser windows or turning off their computer when you enter their room.
- Changes in eating habits, self-harm or suicidal thoughts.
- Acquiring money, clothes or other items for which your teen cannot account.
- Becoming secretive or detached.
- Constantly checking their mobile phone.

Yes, I know, most of these can apply to an average healthy teenager! As a parent you need to be vigilant, but you also need to remain logical. Don't automatically jump to the wrong conclusion. However, if you suspect your teen or another child is being groomed you should contact the police immediately by calling 101 in the UK, or 999 if the offence is taking place at that moment.

ONLINE RADICALISATION
Grooming is not restricted purely to sexual motives. Sometimes young people are targeted online by radical groups attempting to further a political, religious or social ideology. Such groups will attract young people with similar beliefs or motives but can also prey on individuals displaying vulnerabilities or the desire to be recognised and belong.

Although radical groups are prevalent within the dark web, many promote their presence through regular websites and forums available to your teen via a simple Google search. One popular site for radical discussion is Gab.com, which declares itself to be 'the home of free speech online'. Gab, launched in 2017, claims to

➡ Radical groups are utilising the Internet to seek out new members.

have 1 million user accounts and has gained a reputation for harbouring neo-Nazis and white supremacists.

Signs of radicalisation can be similar to those for sexual grooming. However, parents may also note the sudden appearance, or attempted hiding, of certain religious or political publications or an interest in particular activists, websites and videos portraying extremist viewpoints.

An interest in radical issues does not mean your teen is intent on being a part of such activities. That said, most teens simply displaying an innocent interest will probably be more willing to discuss it, so a non-confrontational conversation in the first instance may go a long way towards calming your fears.

⬆ Tracking software can be employed to monitor your teen, but its use may be viewed as a major breach of trust.

If you are concerned your teen is being radicalised

- Listen to your teen. Discuss how they feel, but also how *you* feel and your concerns about their behaviour. Do not expect them to agree with you.
- Let them know they can trust you and that you care, but ensure they have another trusted adult to whom they can turn who isn't a parent. This may be a teacher, youth worker or relative. Your teen will not want to disappoint you and may try to shield you from certain activities or beliefs.
- Seek counselling and support groups so your teen can talk confidentially and without judgement. Support groups will encourage positive activities and can often provide legal advice.
- Ensure your teen's bank account is safe from others. If not, then limit or stop payments to your teen.

- You may wish to monitor your teen's Internet use or use tracking software on a mobile phone. Be forewarned – without doubt this will be viewed by your teen as a *major* breach of trust.
- Don't underestimate the emotional pull on your teen exerted by radical groups. Group mentality provides what sociologists refer to as a plausibility structure, so your teen may feel vindicated in their views as counterarguments are never presented.
- Report illegal activity to the police by calling 101 in the UK. If an act of terrorism is an imminent risk call 999. The government anti-terrorist hotline is contactable on 0800 789 321 or via a confidential web form at www.met.police.uk.

Out with friends

One of the most reassuring stages of your child's development during the teen years is seeing their increasing independence. As any parent will also know, this can be one of the most traumatic stages. While there are no guarantees in life, safety is partly within the control of your teen and requires the same consideration any adult should employ when socialising. Here are some top tips to share with your teen:

- Always stay in a group, preferably of three or more.
- Keep to well-lit areas.
- Always carry a mobile phone and ensure someone knows your planned itinerary, including the time you intend to return home. You can also arrange to call at a certain time to reassure your parent you are safe.
- Carry a personal alarm. They can be discreet and will fit easily into a pocket or bag.
- Resist peer pressure. If others are drinking it doesn't mean you have to. Be prepared to leave a gathering if you feel uneasy about any behaviour.
- Plan your return journey before leaving home.
- Never drink and drive or get into a car with a driver who is under the influence.
- Limit your intake. One unit of alcohol takes an average of one hour for the body to break down. Drugs are illegal wherever they are consumed and are traceable in urine for up to 45 days (depending on the type and quantity of drug).
- Watch drinks being poured, especially if accepting a drink from a stranger. Be aware that any type of drink can be spiked and never leave a drink unattended.

Date rape

For many people the image of rape involves a stranger in a dark place. However, an alarming number of rape cases now occur as part of what is referred to as date rape. The attacker is often known to the victim and both victims and attackers can be male and female. An ONS report for the year ending March 2017 found a staggering 4 million victims were the subject of sexual assault, including over 41,000 cases of rape.

Date rape is often associated with the spiking of drinks. This is achieved by mixing one or more of a number of drugs into the victim's drink. Depending on the drug and the amount administered, the victim may experience disorientation, compromised inhibitions, loss of memory of the attack or even lose consciousness. Spiking, also used as a method to steal from a victim, is punishable by up to ten years in prison.

Common drugs used to spike drinks include Rohypnol, ketamine and GHB (gamma-hydroxybutyric acid). Your teen may not be able to distinguish any change in the colour or taste of their drink, but these are potentially dangerous drugs and their effect can be increased greatly if your teen is taking prescribed medicines or has already ingested alcohol or other drugs. Date rape drugs can take up to 30 minutes to act, so it is not always evident a drink has been spiked. In some cases a victim may willingly take part in drug use but is attacked while compromised under the influence of alcohol or drugs. Whatever the circumstances, the person raped or abused is never to blame. However, there are things your teen can do to protect against date rape and certain recommended steps that can be taken should the worst occur. In addition to the safety points outlined above, your teen should be aware of the following important advice:

Date rape can result from drink spiking.

- Rape and sexual assault can be perpetrated by anyone – male or female, stranger or friend.
- Alcohol often plays a part in rapes and physical attacks. Be aware of how much you are drinking as even a small amount of alcohol can loosen inhibitions and impair responses.
- Don't remain in the company of a person who makes you feel uncomfortable and always stay with a friend or someone you know well.
- Never give personal details to someone you have just met.
- If your partner is drunk or unable to consent to sexual activity it could be *you* that is guilty of rape or sexual assault.
- If you begin to feel unwell, bring this to the attention of a member of staff immediately (if you are in a bar or club) and ensure a trusted friend remains with you while medical assistance is sought.
- If you have been the victim of sexual assault it is vital to contact the police and to keep any evidence such as clothing so DNA samples can be taken.
- Although you cannot be forced to report an incident, it is vital to attend a hospital or surgery to be examined for possible STIs/STDs and pregnancy. If you decide to report a crime it should be done as soon as possible as some drugs leave the body between 12 and 72 hours after ingestion.
- Sexual assaults are not just physical but also carry the risk of long-term emotional scarring. You should be offered the opportunity to discuss the attack with a qualified counsellor. The NHS website provides advice and links to counselling services.

Music

As with many aspects of 21st-century life, music has transformed from how many parents of teens will have initially experienced it. From purchasing and listening to storing to sharing, every aspect has brought new opportunities and new challenges.

Streaming

Perhaps the most significant development has been the ability to stream music. A 2019 record industry report found that, by the end of 2018, 255 million users subscribed to paid streaming services. This won't come as a surprise to your teen, as apps such as Spotify allow free and instant access to almost every album ever produced from the comfort of your own computer or phone. For a monthly fee, users can access enhanced functions such as improved sound quality and the ability to download and store music to a computer or phone.

While Spotify is currently the dominant streaming site (with over 271 million monthly active users worldwide), sites such as Pandora, TIDAL and Soundcloud are also very popular – each catering for a slightly different user base. For example, Soundcloud is a streaming site hosting

⬇ The Internet has transformed all aspects of the music business.

user-generated content and is aimed at amateur musicians.

Streaming, whether through music-specific sites or video apps such as YouTube, has made it much harder for parents to monitor or control what their children are listening to, although some apps such as Deezer allow parents to set an age filter to block explicit content.

Downloads

Downloads are usually songs or albums purchased through a website or app that are then owned by the person downloading and remain on their computer or phone without any expiration date. Downloading was

⬇ Spotify is currently the market leader in music streaming with over 271 million monthly users.

popular in the early days of online music, but its use has decreased significantly with the advent of streaming.

Free trials

As with most modern resources on the Internet, music products are usually free for a trial period or for an app with limited features. Your teen may be required to pay a monthly fee in order to receive the ability to listen without random shuffling of tracks, or to hear music streamed at a higher bitrate with superior quality audio. It is important your teen understands the terms and conditions to which they are agreeing when subscribing to a service as it will often be their responsibility to cancel a subscription within a limited time period if they wish to avoid paying a monthly subscription fee.

Chapter 4

Drugs, alcohol and tobacco

If ever there's an emotive subject for teens, and many adults, it's around the rights and wrongs of drugs.

It probably comes as no surprise to learn the most commonly used drug in the UK is caffeine, closely followed by alcohol and nicotine. In fact these have become so ingrained in everyday society many people don't consider them under the label of drugs. Even the word 'drug' causes confusion as it can refer to 'any natural or artificially made chemical that is used as medicine' in addition to 'a chemical or other substance that is illegally used, sometimes to improve performance in an activity or because someone cannot stop using it'. However, it is probably fair to say when parents have concerns about drugs it is rarely around those prescribed by a GP.

Young people and drug use

Although it is not possible to determine the exact number of young people using illegal drugs, statistics from a 2019 Home Office survey for England and Wales show slightly over 1 in 5 people aged 16–24 had used illegal drugs in the previous 12 months and that approximately 1 in 9 people aged 16–24 had taken a drug in the previous month.

The latest NHS figures on drug misuse in England (2018) found 24% of pupils had admitted taking drugs and the likelihood of having taken drugs increased with age, from 11% of 11-year-olds to 37% of 15-year-olds.

The most popular illegal drug for young people is cannabis, followed by nitrous oxide and cocaine.

Cannabis. Changes to cannabis legislation since the beginning of the century have led to confusion among many adults and young people as to its legal status. Cannabis was reclassified from class B to class C in January 2004, removing the threat of arrest for possession at a time when 49% of British adults supported its decriminalisation. This allowed police forces to concentrate their resources on tackling 'harder drugs'. However, in January 2009 cannabis was reclassified as class B. Cannabis legislation is sometimes unheeded by young people, possibly as it has become ubiquitous within youth culture and an increasing

It is also possible, but less common, to inject a solution of cocaine.

Ketamine is used medically as an anaesthetic. When taken illegally it is usually in the form of a white powder that is swallowed, injected or snorted, and acts as a hallucinogen.

number of countries have moved to decriminalise its use, including several states in the USA.

Nitrous oxide, also known as laughing gas, is a colourless gas often inhaled via small metal canisters or balloons. Intake can cause a range of emotions from euphoria or calmness to paranoia and the risks can be severe and even fatal. There is no penalty for possession of nitrous oxide, however it is illegal to give away or sell.

Cocaine is the second most popular illegal drug used by adults and acts as a strong stimulant. It is taken either as a powder (coke), freebase (a crystallised powder) or smoked as a small rock (crack).

MDMA is a powder commonly referred to by its American slang-name of Molly. However, it is probably best known by parents in its pill form as ecstasy. While most users will experience a heightened state of energy and affection for those around them, others may experience paranoia or anxiety. The high will usually last for 2–4 hours, although as with all drugs, this will depend heavily on the physical make-up of each user and the purity of the dose.

Other popular recreational drugs include (so-called) legal highs, manufactured to mimic the effects of other drugs, and Spice. Legal highs (also referred to as new psychoactive substances) are a misnomer as they now fall under the 2016 Psychoactive Substances Act. As such they are illegal to give away or sell, and while there is no penalty for possession (unless in custody), supply or production can incur up to seven years in prison and an unlimited fine. According to the Office for National Statistics, 125 deaths were attributed to the consumption of new psychoactive substances in 2018.

Spice refers to a plant-based drug mixed with synthetic chemicals. It acts in a similar way to cannabis but is much more potent, with one police and crime commissioner stating in 2018 that Spice was the 'most severe public health issue we have faced in decades'.

The law

Illegal drugs are placed within three classes, A to C, with class A drugs carrying the greatest penalties for possession, supply and production. The table below details these drugs and the associated penalties.

Class	Drug	Possession	Supply and production
A	Crack cocaine, cocaine, ecstasy (MDMA), heroin, LSD, magic mushrooms, methadone, methamphetamine (crystal meth)	Up to 7 years in prison, an unlimited fine or both	Up to life in prison, an unlimited fine or both
B	Amphetamines, barbiturates, cannabis, codeine, ketamine, methylphenidate (Ritalin), synthetic cannabinoids, synthetic cathinones (for example mephedrone, methoxetamine)	Up to 5 years in prison, an unlimited fine or both	Up to 14 years in prison, an unlimited fine or both
C	Anabolic steroids, benzodiazepines (diazepam), gamma hydroxybutyrate (GHB), gamma-butyrolactone (GBL), piperazines (BZP), khat	Up to 2 years in prison, an unlimited fine or both (except anabolic steroids – it's not an offence to possess them for personal use)	Up to 14 years in prison, an unlimited fine or both
Temporary class drugs*	Some methylphenidate substances (ethylphenidate, 3,4-dichloromethylphenidate (3,4-DCMP), methylnaphthidate (HDMP-28), isopropylphenidate (IPP or IPPD), 4-methylmethylphenidate, ethylnaphthidate, propylphenidate (and their simple derivatives)	None, but police can take away a suspected temporary class drug	Up to 14 years in prison, an unlimited fine or both

PSYCHOACTIVE SUBSTANCES PENALTIES

Psychoactive substances include things like nitrous oxide ('laughing gas')

You can get a fine or prison sentence if you:
- carry a psychoactive substance and you intend to supply it
- make a psychoactive substance
- sell, deal or share a psychoactive substance (also called supplying them)

Psychoactive substances	Possession	Supply and production
Things that cause hallucinations, drowsiness or changes in alertness, perception of time and space, mood or empathy with others	None, unless you're in prison	Up to 7 years in prison, an unlimited fine or both
Food, alcohol, nicotine, caffeine, medicine and the types of drugs listed above do not count as psychoactive substances		

Issues to consider if using illegal drugs

- All drugs carry a risk of side effects. Most will have an effect on the heart, blood pressure and respiration. Risks vary depending on the individual user and in extreme cases can prove fatal.
- Illegal drugs are unregulated, therefore it's impossible to know the strength of drugs being ingested, regardless of whether they are purchased from a regular dealer or manufacturer.
- Drugs are almost always 'cut' with other substances (many of which are highly toxic) in order to bulk out the weight and increase profits for the dealer. It is possible drugs have been cut several times before they are consumed.
- A drug conviction may not be wiped when a young person reaches the age of 18. This can severely damage employment opportunities, especially if applying for work with, or around, vulnerable people such as the young, old and infirm.
- A drug conviction can prevent travel to other countries and an applicant securing a mortgage and most types of insurance.
- Possession of an illegal substance can lead to prosecution, regardless of whether you are the owner.
- Police take seriously the possession and use of all illegal drugs. They can issue a warning or on-the-spot fine of £90 if you are in possession of cannabis.
- If you are adamant on carrying illegal substances you should ensure you do not carry an amount that can be regarded by police or the courts as intent to supply.
- Drug laws change periodically, including changes in the classification of certain drugs. These can affect penalties for possession, supply and production.
- If you are under 18, police can inform your parent(s), guardian(s) or carer(s) if you have been caught in the possession of drugs.

The culture surrounding drug use

Every parent will have seen scare stories in the media about young people and drugs. It is certainly a fact that no town, village or city is immune to drugs and a dealer is only a phone call away. Illegal drugs can even be delivered to your door via the dark net.

If your teen hasn't dabbled with illegal substances, there is a good chance several of their peers have. As such, your teen may be under pressure to participate.

Peer pressure is still the most significant factor in young people experimenting with drugs, although some young people will also self-medicate with illegal drugs to mask physical or emotional issues.

As a parent it is important you stay informed of trends in drug use, some of which may be specific to your home location. New forms of drugs appear on a

➡ **Possession of cannabis can result in your teen receiving an on-the-spot fine.**

regular basis and many are also known by slang names that change as they fall in and out of fashion. Pseudonyms for most drugs can be found on drug awareness sites such as Frank. It may be helpful to create an opportunity for a calm and informal chat with your teen about drugs and peer pressure. Your teen's school will almost certainly be doing the same as part of its PSHE curriculum, but it's important your teen is aware of your concerns and that you are available for support if required.

One particularly troubling aspect of young people being pressured into drug activity relates to county lines.

County lines

County lines has become a hot topic in the media, and not without justification. It refers to activity in which drug dealers expand their trade into smaller towns and villages by exploiting young and vulnerable people as dealers and runners. One common practice is 'cuckooing', by which dealers will take over a vulnerable person's property to use as a 'trap house' for their dealing or production activities.

Although it's not possible to know exactly how many young people are involved in county lines, the Children's Commissioner estimates approximately 4,000 teenagers in London alone. A number of these will have been groomed into county lines activity, often through the gifting of money, electronic goods and drugs or the façade of friendship. If young people are drug users themselves, they may build up arrears to the dealers and be caught in a spiralling cycle of debt. Sometimes young people are even forced to participate through physical or sexual violence or threats to themselves or their family.

⬇ County Lines often exploit the young and vulnerable to move drugs around the country.

Signs your teen may be being groomed for county lines activities are similar to other forms of grooming. These may include:

- A change to their routine, including staying out late or periods when they go missing.
- A change in their behaviour, possibly exhibiting signs of anxiety or depression.
- Unexplained injuries.
- Secretive conversations and locked drawers or containers.
- Travel to new places without good reason.
- Being in possession of new clothes, money or goods for which they can't explain.
- Unexplained absences from school or work.
- Possession of a second mobile phone, unexplained keys or hotel cards.

- A new group of friends or acquaintances, or regular visitors or new tenants in a particular property.
- Being transported by persons unknown to you.

If you are concerned your teen may be in danger you should speak in the first instance to the police by calling 101 in the UK. Anonymous information can be given to the police via the charity Crimestoppers by calling 0800 555 111.

While young people can also call these numbers, they may wish to discuss any concerns with Childline on 0800 1111 or a trusted adult such as a youth worker or teacher. Don't expect your teen to open up to you as they may be feeling embarrassed or anxious about threats made towards their family.

⬇ Possession of a second mobile phone may be cause for concern.

Alcohol

The average age for first consuming a whole alcoholic drink is 13 and consumption is usually within a family setting. While this may appear preferential to your teen drinking with their peers outside the home, research shows a strong correlation between the attitude of parents and the onset of drinking in teens.

The NHS found young people aged 11–15 in England are more inclined to drink if they live with other people who drink alcohol. Some 79% of pupils who did not live with anyone who drank alcohol had never drunk alcohol themselves, compared with 31% of pupils who lived with three or more drinkers. The same report found parents' views towards alcohol also play a significant part in influencing their children's attitudes, claiming, 'Of pupils who had never drunk alcohol, three-quarters (75%) said that their parents would not like them to drink. 86% of pupils who had drunk in the last week said that their parents did not mind them drinking as long as they didn't drink too much.'

Some parents make a conscious decision to let their children try alcohol, often under the pretence this will instil a more responsible attitude in later life. However, there is no scientific evidence to back this theory. In fact, one study by the US government found young people who started drinking before the age of 15 were four times more likely to become alcohol-dependent later in their lives.

It may come as a surprise to learn it is perfectly legal in the UK to let children drink alcohol in their home from the age of 5! Unsurprisingly there is a wealth of evidence that points to this being unwise. Alcohol consumption can be dangerous to a child's health and inhibits the development of organs, bone growth, hormones and brain function. It is further linked to an increased risk of mental health issues, suicidal tendencies, risky sexual behaviour and violence. The fact that alcohol is responsible for approximately 20 deaths a day in the UK should also be a sobering statistic for your teen. Long-term health implications related to alcohol are well documented, but fortunately deaths among young people due to alcohol poisoning are extremely rare. Deaths that do involve young people and alcohol are usually associated with other factors such as driving under the influence.

⬆ Studies have shown children of drinkers are more likely to be alcohol dependent later in life.

NHS advice is to restrict alcohol consumption to persons of at least 15 years of age or older and that your teen only drinks rarely. As you would probably expect, there are increased dangers from binge drinking, the practice of drinking large amounts of alcohol within a short period of time. In the UK this is defined as 8 units of alcohol in a single session for a man and 6 units for a woman. An NHS report published in 2019 found English pupils who drank alcohol within the week prior to being questioned consumed an average of 6 units. This figure rises sharply with age. A 2016 survey found alcohol consumption in the UK amounted to an average consumption of 22 units of alcohol per week for those aged 15 years and

⬅ An increasing number of young people are opting to be teetotal.

older. To put this in context, current government guidelines suggest the consumption of no more than 14 units of alcohol each week for men and women.

Although motives behind drinking will be unique to each individual, young people believe the reason most people of their age drink is to look cool in front of their friends (74%), to be more sociable with friends (63%), because it gives them a rush (63%) or because their friends pressure them into it (61%). Whatever the reasons for drinking, there exists strict legislation as to drinking ages in the UK. Your teen can be stopped, fined or arrested if they are under 18 and drinking alcohol in a public place. If under 18 they are unable to buy or attempt to buy alcohol and it is an offence for someone to sell it to them or to buy it on their behalf. The only circumstance in which they can consume alcohol in licensed premises is if they are 16 or 17, accompanied by an adult and consuming a drink of beer, cider or wine with a meal. Full guidance around current legislation can be found on the government website.

How you can support your teen's relationship with alcohol

- Model good practice.
- Take time to maintain a relaxed and open dialogue with your teen around the issue of alcohol. Make it clear as to what age you will allow them to consume alcohol in the home.
- You may choose to resist your teen's requests to let them finish your drink or to try alcohol. If you decide to let your teen drink, be aware of the strength of different brands of alcohol and do not allow them to drink spirits.
- Keep bottles of alcohol securely locked away.
- If your teen is already drinking against your wishes, let them know you disapprove and will not tolerate such behaviour in the house.
- Be ready to support your teen with sound advice and guidance. The NHS website provides professional and comprehensive guidance.

- Ensure your teen understands the dangers of mixing drinks and of drink spiking.
- Reassure your teen they do not have to succumb to peer pressure and can choose soft drinks, or switch to soft drinks after an alcoholic drink.
- Do not aid and abet your teen's activities by purchasing alcohol for them to take to a party.
- If you or your teen is concerned about their level of alcohol consumption you should discuss concerns with a GP. They will be able to inform you of the best course of action and signpost appropriate support agencies.
- Most importantly, try not to panic. Alcohol is a rite of passage for many young people. Most will adjust to a sensible attitude towards drinking and an increasing number are even opting to be teetotal.

Tobacco

The dangers of smoking are no longer something hidden away by governments and cigarette manufacturers. They are well documented and the toll on public health is catastrophic. According to the NHS, 'smoking is the biggest cause of preventable deaths in England, accounting for nearly 80,000 deaths each year', and half of all smokers will die from the result of their smoking.

A survey of secondary school pupils in years 7–11 (Smoking, Drinking and Drug Use among Young People) is carried out every two years and published by NHS Digital. The latest survey, published in August 2019, found 16% of pupils had tried smoking at least once, 5% were current smokers and 2% were regular smokers. Regular smoking increased with age; from less than 1% of 11- and 12-year-olds, to 5% of 15-year-olds.

As with alcohol, parental behaviour is a significant factor as to how teens behave,

with young people more likely to smoke if they live in a house with smokers. Those with parents or siblings who smoke are approximately three times as likely to smoke than those from non-smoking homes.

The laws around smoking can be confusing for parents and teens alike. Although the police have the right to confiscate cigarettes from under-16s in public areas and the age limit to purchase cigarettes has increased to 18, it is still legal for young people to smoke at any age in private.

➡ Roll-your-own cigarettes carry a greater risk of some cancers than pre-rolled cigarettes.

Both traditional boxed cigarettes (usually filtered and sometimes referred to as straights), and roll-up cigarettes (also referred to as roll your own or RYO) are popular with young people. The most common reasons for smoking roll-up cigarettes is that they are cheaper, tobacco can be rationed according to the wish of the user, and they can be combined easily with cannabis or other drugs. Some young people consider roll-ups to be healthier, however this is not the case. Roll-ups contain 4,000 toxic chemicals and carry the same health risks (including cancer, stroke, heart and lung disease, impotence and infertility) as pre-packaged cigarettes. In fact roll-up cigarettes actually carry a greater risk of some cancers of the mouth, oesophagus, pharynx and larynx compared to pre-packaged and filtered cigarettes.

Secondary smoking

Even for non-smokers there are health risks through the inhalation of secondary smoke, also known as second-hand smoke or passive smoking. This can be the cause of numerous health concerns, ranging from short-term headaches and sore throats to long-term issues such as heart disease, respiratory issues, lung cancer and stroke. Second-hand smoke is

⬇ Passive smoking around minors is illegal in a car, but lawful in the home.

particularly hazardous within enclosed spaces.

In a 2016 NHS survey, 57% of young people were found to have been exposed to second-hand smoke in their home and 25% in a car. Although it is legal to smoke at home when minors are present, since October 2015 it has been illegal to smoke in a car when someone under the age of 18 is being transported.

E-cigarettes/vapes

A relatively recent alternative to traditional smoking has been the advent of e-cigarettes. The smoking of e-cigarettes, or vaping, has grown in popularity year on year, largely due to offering a way of weaning oneself from the dangers of traditional cigarettes. A quarter of pupils surveyed said they had used e-cigarettes, although regular e-cigarette usage is low at 2%.

With e-cigarettes the user inhales a vapour as opposed to smoke. They are free of tobacco, tar and carbon monoxide, but often contain nicotine. However, does that make vaping a healthy, or healthier,

⬇ Although not entirely safe, vapes are considered to be a healthier option compared to traditional cigarettes.

option compared to smoking traditional cigarettes? Although research into e-cigarettes is still at a very early stage, health professionals are largely of the impression vaping is a significantly healthier option compared to traditional cigarettes. In fact research by a number of reputable health bodies, including Public Health England, estimate vapes are at least 95% less harmful. There is also currently no evidence that vaping is dangerous for those nearby in the way that second-hand smoke from traditional cigarettes can be harmful to health.

So far, so good. However, this does not mean vaping is entirely without risks. Although e-cigarettes do not contain tobacco, they do heat a solution that may contain nicotine along with propylene glycol (a colourless synthetic sometimes used as a food additive), tetrahydrocannabinol (THC), cannabinoid (CBD) oils and other chemicals. There have been numerous reports around the world of respiratory issues, lung disease and even deaths resulting from vaping. In fact some countries have gone as far as banning e-cigarettes or solutions containing certain flavourings or scents. Although the UK National Institute for Health Research found vaping to be twice as effective at helping smokers quit compared to alternative methods, there remains the risk that vaping, with its reduced health risks and myriad options around flavours and additives, may actually be a step into smoking, and even towards traditional cigarettes, for those who currently abstain. And if all the above isn't enough to deter your teen from smoking, even at a very practical level concerns continue to be raised around potential burn and fire risks due to e-cigarettes and their chargers overheating and exploding.

How to challenge teen smoking

■ As with all attempts to support your teen, you should lead by example. If you are a smoker then be prepared to reduce or stop your smoking.

■ Do not fund your teen's smoking. You may, however, choose to reward them for *not* smoking.

■ Encourage your teen to place money that would have been spent on cigarettes into a bank account and watch it accrue. A target can be set of a certain level of savings and a treat can possibly be chosen by your teen as an incentive.

■ Find healthy substitutes for cigarettes. Be wary of replacing cigarettes with junk food.

■ Assist your teen in keeping a record of when cravings worsen. Is there a recognisable pattern – maybe linked with mealtimes or stressful situations?

■ Urging your teen to stay away from their smoking peers is probably a wasted effort. However, they may actually relish the opportunity to demonstrate their independent nature and willpower in front of their friends!

■ Exercise! Studies have shown exercise helps your brain produce anti-craving chemicals.

■ Consult with a GP or other health professional as to the best way to reduce or stop smoking.

■ Explore the option of vaping if you or your teen are currently smoking traditional cigarettes. They are not 100% safe, but many health professionals claim they are a significantly healthier option compared to tobacco.

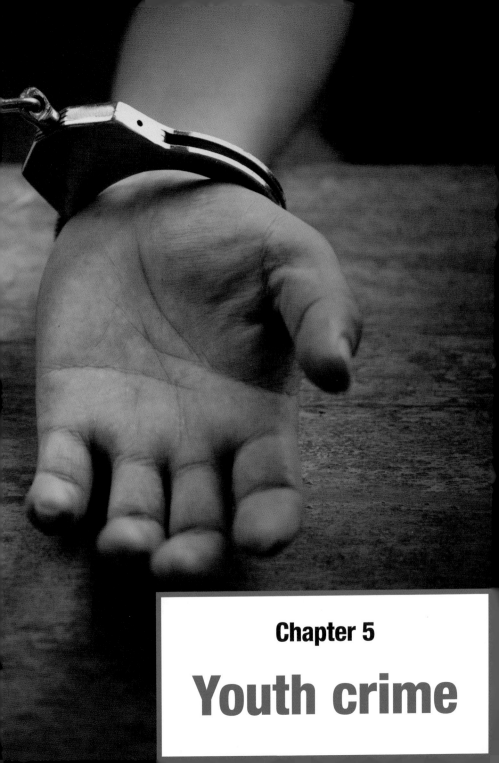

Chapter 5

Youth crime

Most parents will have concerns at some point about their child's friendship group and a number of these concerns will focus on the risk of criminal behaviour.

While the vast majority of young people are a lot more sensible and law-abiding than media would have us believe, that's not to say bad things don't happen, and at first glance the figures make for grim reading. A government report for 2017–18 shows 70,300 offences committed by young people; 76% of these were committed by 15- to 17-year-olds and 84% were committed by males. By far the largest number of offences were classified as violence against the person and the (known) rate at which people reoffended was 40.9%. Although it is difficult to pinpoint the exact cause of

every criminal act, research has identified certain factors that increase the likelihood of experiencing crime, with young adults, males, the unemployed and those living in rented housing and more deprived areas experiencing the greatest risk.

Although the UK is a comparatively safe country, nowhere can be considered immune to street violence. However, it's not all bad news. The fear of being the victim of crime is significantly greater than the actual rate of incidents. In 2017 the ONS attempted to alleviate concerns by releasing research showing 0.3% of adults were victims of robbery in the year ending March 2016, despite 9% expressing fear they would be a victim.

⬇ Keep to well-lit areas and avoid underpasses where possible.

Steps your teen can take to help them stay safe

- Keep to well-lit areas and avoid underpasses where possible.
- Always travel in a group, preferably with at least two others.
- Remain sober.
- Avoid strangers. Take a safe detour if concerned about individuals or groups. If you do converse with strangers, never reveal personal details.
- If you are bothered by someone who refuses to leave you alone, alert other people. Be loud and confident in your tone.
- Avoid wearing headphones. They both suppress the sound of those around you and advertise you are carrying a phone or other electronic device.
- Arrange transport to and from home if necessary and only use official taxi services.
- Do not retaliate if threatened. It is much wiser to lose your belongings than risk your personal safety.
- Consider a code word that can be used in difficult situations whether around a friend or in contact with your family.
- Have a key ready to unlock your front door rather than fumbling for keys on a doorstep.
- Ensure bags are secured and if possible that openings are turned against your body.
- Carry purses and wallets zipped on the inside of a coat.
- Consider carrying a second wallet containing a small amount of money and old cards to hand over if you are the victim of mugging.

⬇ Keep all bags secured, preferably with fastenings facing the body.

Drug dealing

A key factor in young people turning to crime is drugs. This can be to fund a habit, to make money through production or dealing or as the result of gang involvement. Gang involvement can be the result of peer pressure, bravado or forced participation in activities such as county lines.

It is important to realise that any activity concerning illegal drugs involves your teen breaking the law and makes them susceptible to a criminal record, fines and imprisonment. For possible signs your teen may be involved with drugs or county lines activities, refer to Chapter Four.

Gang culture

It is sometimes tempting as an adult to perceive any group of young people as a gang without acknowledging the difficulty they face in finding a safe and age-appropriate meeting space outside their home. A 2010 government paper attempted to establish a clear distinction between groups of young people:

- **Peer groups** – a relatively small and transient social grouping which may or may not describe themselves as a gang depending on the context.
- **Street gangs** – groups of young people who see themselves (and are seen by others) as a discernible group for whom crime and violence is integral to the group's identity.
- **Organised criminal gangs** – a group of individuals for whom involvement in crime is for personal gain (financial or otherwise).

⬇ Groups of young people are often unfairly perceived as a gang.

The real extent of street gangs is different to how media often portrays the topic, although there are significant variances in membership depending on location. ONS data published in 2018 found 0.7% of 10- to 15-year-olds in England and Wales claimed to belong to a street gang in 2016–17 and 0.2% of 16- to 24-year-olds. A 2019 Children's Commissioner report stated 27,000 children in England identify as a gang member, and that many more are on the periphery of gang membership.

⬆ Some young people are keen to escape gang culture but are afraid of repercussions for themselves and their families.

WHY DO YOUNG PEOPLE JOIN GANGS?

There is no single reason why young people belong to gangs. However, common themes include:

- Feeling accepted, loved, protected and part of a family, especially if they feel neglected or abused by their biological family.
- Repaying a debt bond. Young people who lose a gang's illicit money or drugs through arrest or theft become indebted to the gang and are forced into continued service to pay off their debt.
- Seeking excitement.
- A common interest in an activity or territory.
- Gaining status and respect or benefiting financially.
- Succumbing to peer pressure.

It is interesting to note a well-organised gang not only works along the same lines as a productive family or organisation, offering rules, authority, boundaries and maybe even a uniform, but also appears, at least at face value, to offer all of the elements of Maslow's hierarchy of needs. It should therefore come as no surprise that many young people, especially the vulnerable or abused, are so enticed by gang culture.

SHOULD I WORRY?

Depending on the type of gang into which your teen is drawn, the answer could be yes. The Children's Commissioner defined criminal gangs operating in England as, 'complex and ruthless organisations, which use sophisticated techniques to groom children and chilling levels of violence to keep them compliant'. She further noted children in gangs, even compared with other vulnerable children referred to children's services, are:

- 95% more likely to have social and emotional health issues.
- More than twice as likely to be self-harming.
- 41% more likely to have a parent or carer misusing substances.
- Eight times more likely to be misusing substances themselves.

How you can support your teen

- Be aware of possible signs of gang membership. These can be similar to those for grooming, radicalisation and drug abuse. A further sign may be that your teen is very particular about clothing, especially wearing or omitting certain colours. (Though that includes just about every teenager.)
- Talk to your teen about possible gang involvement. Try to remain calm and reasoned. Listen to their opinions but also explain why you are concerned and let them know you love them and are available to talk. Remember, being in a gang isn't against the law. However, gang activity *may* involve illegal activities.
- Offer your support. Your teen may be seeking a way out but is unsure as to where to turn, especially if they're feeling threatened. Confidential support is also available via Childline and Gangsline.
- If you are aware of criminal behaviour you may wish to call Crimestoppers on 0800 555 111 (in the UK) to give confidential information.
- It may be useful to discuss concerns with your teen's school-appointed safeguarding officer, a youth worker or the police.
- Encourage your teen to be proactive by changing friendship groups, participating in positive activities and avoiding areas where they know gangs are present.

Knife crime

In recent years knife crime has become a particularly high-profile concern across the UK. In the year ending March 2019, there were around 47,100 offences involving a knife or sharp instrument recorded in England and Wales, the highest number since records began. Roughly 20% of these offences involved young people.

There are several reasons why young people carry knives, including personal protection, deprivation (particularly in cases of serious violence), poor mental health and peer/gang pressure. However, it is vital for your teen to understand that carrying a knife in a public place (without 'lawful authority or reasonable excuse') is a possible offence under Section 1 of the Prevention of Crime Act 1953 as it can be deemed an offensive weapon. The Act defines an offensive weapon as 'any article made or adapted for use for causing injury

← The level of knife crime has risen dramatically in the UK.

to the person, or intended by the person having it with him for such use by him or by some other person'.

Not only does carrying a knife risk your teen receiving a criminal record, it also makes them more vulnerable to serious harm. One research into knife crime found victims of knife crime were 'twice as likely to carry a knife themselves compared to non-victims'.

Gun crime

If ever there can be said to be good news on gun crime, it is that overall gun crime in England and Wales is on the decrease. However, a 2018 report published by the London Assembly Police and Crime Committee also found a significant rise in gun crime in London over the previous three years, principally as the result of drug and gang activity. In fact, gang activity accounted for almost half of all offences where a fatality was caused due to firearms. Some 96% of perpetrators were male and likewise males accounted for 65% of victims. Women and girls often

⬆ Gun-related crimes are still rare in the UK.

⬇ There is no minimum age for holding a shotgun licence in the UK.

took on the role as holders of weapons as it was assumed, erroneously, they would receive more lenient sentences if caught. The result of this activity was 29 homicide victims killed by shooting in the year ending March 2018. As distressing as this figure may first appear, it needs to be placed in context compared to the USA where deaths related to firearms in 2019 totalled a staggering 39,423.

One reason for the relatively low level of gun crime in the UK is the strict legislation around gun ownership. You must be 18 to purchase a firearm. Although this is the same age as for purchasing a knife in the UK, the obvious difference is that guns are not a typical feature of the average UK home. This is in stark contrast to the USA where approximately 40% of Americans say they own a gun or live in a household containing one. You have to be 14 years of age before you can apply for a firearms certificate, although there is no minimum age for a shotgun certificate. Young people aged 14–17 are not allowed to purchase, hire or be gifted an airgun or ammunition; however, they are permitted to borrow an airgun from someone over 18 for use on private property with the property owner's consent. Handguns were banned in Great Britain following the Dunblane school massacre in 1996, although this ban does not apply to Northern Ireland. Detailed information on firearms legislation can be found on the government's website.

Illegal street racing and car cruising

Street racing is an illegal activity, unless held on closed roads and with consent of the police. Hailing from the American drag racing of the 1950s and bolstered by video games and the *Fast and Furious* film franchise, street racing appeals mostly to young males. They are attracted primarily by their common interest in souped-up cars, but race for a variety of reasons:

⬇ Street racing is an illegal activity, unless held on closed roads and with consent of the police.

- The thrill of an unregulated environment.
- The lack of financial outlay and noise restrictions compared to using a racetrack.
- A community bonding experience.
- To show off their vehicle and prove its superiority over another vehicle.
- To taunt police and other authorities.
- As a form of gambling.

The potential danger posed to the public, property and drivers is substantial. Few of the vehicles are equipped with roll bars and most drivers lack even rudimentary fire-retardant clothing or helmets. Cars are almost always adapted by tuning, or using nitrous oxide, turbos and aftermarket exhausts. It is important for your teen to understand any such change to a vehicle must be declared to an insurance company and will invariably lead to greatly inflated insurance premiums. No insurance policy will cover illegal street-racing activities, so many young people make the decision to drive without appropriate insurance.

A 'car cruise' refers to a gathering of car enthusiasts, sometimes numbering in the thousands, who meet to show their cars. Meetings often take place within a large tarmacked area such as a car park or along high-profile carriageways. Cruising is not illegal and some organised car cruises have the approval of police and local councils. Car cruising gatherings are treated on a case-by-case basis by different police forces. Some forces may deem gatherings to be an act of anti-social behaviour and will ask groups to disperse.

Supporting your teen

It is vital for any teen driving a vehicle to be in possession of appropriate legal

⬆ Even a decal added to your teen's car can invalidate their insurance.

documents, including a valid licence, insurance, tax and MOT. Any changes or additions to the car made after it was produced should be declared to the insurance company. These can include stickers/decals to the bodywork, tuning, brakes, spoilers and other body kit and changes to exhausts, lights and wheels.

Your teen should be aware any prosecution will not only incur punishment for that particular infringement but may also affect their chance of securing *any* type of insurance or mortgage in the future as well as possibly affecting their employment opportunities.

It is wise to have an open dialogue with your teen around all aspects of motor vehicle ownership, preferably before they hit the legal age for driving or riding. If you are funding or part-funding their purchase or any additional costs involved with car or bike ownership, then make it clear you will only fund legal pursuits. If your teen is still adamant about pursuing racing activities, there may be value in exploring legal outlets for their need for speed such as stock car racing, rallying or karting.

Chapter 6

Staying healthy

Personal hygiene

Talking about health and a healthy lifestyle with your teen can be an uphill struggle. You can possibly still remember back to a time when you were convinced of your own immortality and that old age was something that only happened to – well – old people!

However, even though many young people are shielded from some of the less pleasant aspects of life, they are still subject to their own mini nightmare as puberty heralds sweat pores, oily skin and acne. While personal hygiene should be a concern for people of any age, in a classroom environment even a temporary flaw in your teen's hygiene can lead to years of merciless persecution and bullying.

Good hygiene practice will come as no surprise to most teens, but for some it may require modelling from a parent. You should try to ensure your teen:

⬇ Teen years herald the nightmare of greasy skin and oily hair.

- Has access to (and wears) clean clothing, including changing underwear daily.
- Bathes or showers daily and after any physical activity. Puberty stimulates your teen's sweat glands leading to excretion of chemicals with a strong odour.
- Washes their hair regularly. Puberty increases the secretion from sebaceous glands leading to greasy hair.
- Applies deodorant and anti-perspirant.
- Cleans their teeth at least twice a day. Brushing, flossing and using mouthwash should be routine, as well as regular check-ups with their dentist. Avoiding sugary drinks and tea/coffee can reduce tooth decay, staining and help avoid bad breath.

Don't forget that as a parent it is your duty to ensure clean clothing is available along with supplies of hygiene products. For girls this will include securing access to sanitary products. If you expect your teen to

↑ Don't assume your teen knows how to care for their health.

finance these from an allowance, ensure you have discussed your teen's needs and they are receiving sufficient payment to cover their costs. You can further assist by ensuring bedding is washed regularly, avoiding fibres in bedding and clothing that aggravate your teen's skin and cleaning up hairs and other detritus left behind by family pets.

Refusers!

It's easy as an adult to forget that younger children don't sweat to the same extent as teens going through puberty. If some gentle coaxing is required to point your teen towards personal hygiene, then ensure you don't go in heavy! You are not attempting to give them a complex for the rest of their life, but they do need to realise they function as part of a family and social group. It may be appropriate for the subject to be broached

by another trusted adult, sibling or peer. Alternatively, your teen could be guided towards an age-appropriate pamphlet or website. Don't expect your teen to read a whole book on hygiene. I imagine even health professionals would baulk at that prospect!

As any parent will know all too well, sometimes the best persuasion of parents or peers is still not enough to bring about change. You may need to consider if there is a reason why your teen is neglecting their hygiene. Discuss your concerns in private with your teen's school to explore any underlying issues and if the subject has already been broached with your teen. A health professional may also be consulted.

Model good practice in your own daily routine and don't take for granted that your teen understands the correct way to apply deodorants, use sanitary products or to shave, brush and floss. More specific hygiene issues should always be addressed by consulting a GP as they may be the result of an infection or other medical condition, such as hyperhidrosis which causes excessive sweating. In extreme cases inadequate hygiene can be symptomatic of other issues – a poor state of mental health or as the result of a traumatic experience such as sexual abuse or unwanted attention.

Personal hygiene is just one consideration within a wider programme that should include exercise, diet and mental well-being.

Exercise

Exercise is perhaps the most 'Marmite' topic of all. While to some it is an essential part of the daily routine, to others it is undertaken only under duress as part of a school curriculum. It is important for your teen to realise not only that exercise should go hand in hand with a healthy diet, but that exercise can take many forms and is also conducive to good mental health.

It may be tempting to believe the online lifestyle of the 21st century has turned all teens into sedentary purveyors of phones and computer monitors. While this is far from the true picture, research does show some cause for concern. One such concern relates to the rising obesity level among young people. It is difficult to calculate the number of obese teenagers as official recording of height and weight stops after year 6. However, the 2017/18 figures for year 6 pupils (aged 10 to 11 years) revealed one in five children was obese. A 2019 government briefing paper further found that boys are more likely to be obese, as are children living in deprived areas. These are troubling statistics as childhood obesity is associated with numerous health risks, including cardiovascular diseases, asthma, early-onset type-2 diabetes and mental health issues and can lead to a sedentary lifestyle as an adult.

How much exercise should my teen get?

The NHS recommends young people participate in 'an average of at least 60 minutes of moderate-intensity physical activity a day across the week'. However, only 17.5% of young people are classed as achieving the recommended level.

Several factors can influence your teen's enthusiasm for exercise, including:

- A dislike of team or competitive sports.
- A perception of failing or not being good enough at an activity.
- Lack of access to facilities.
- Financial outlay.

➡ Teenage obesity levels are on the rise.

- Changes in temperature.
- Embarrassment due to their current physical condition.
- Peer pressure.
- Time pressures such as clubs, homework or household chores.
- Negative perceptions about gym environments.

⬇ Teenagers should aim for at least an hour of physical activity each day.

Although moderate activity should make your teen breathe faster and feel warmer,

activities do not have to revolve around traditional or team sports. Walking to school, skateboarding, dog walking and cycling are all beneficial forms of exercise. The NHS recommends that for three days a week, activities focus on building muscles and bones. Suitable activities for teens include traditional school team sports such as football, hockey, basketball and netball as well as gymnastics, rock climbing, running and martial arts.

It is important for your teen to realise that calories can be burned through any form of activity, although some forms of

↑ Exercise isn't restricted to running or school sports.

exercise burn calories at a much higher rate and are more conducive to heart health and weight loss. An extensive list detailing the rate at which calories are burned as the result of different activities (from running to sitting in a classroom) can be found on the Harvard Health Publishing website.

As with all exercise- and health-related pursuits, appropriate activities and exertion levels will vary from individual to individual. Professional medical advice should always be sought via your GP if you or your teen are in any doubt as to the suitability of an activity.

How can I support my teen?

As with most aspects of life, the best way to encourage positive activity is to model it. If you are unable to value exercise and find time in your busy diary, don't expect your teen to value it and find time either.

Attending a sports match could be part of your activities to bolster your teen's enthusiasm for an active lifestyle. You may also find they will be willing to join you for a run or as part of a gym session. Alternatively, you could explore options for teen-only gym sessions (usually available immediately after school hours) or you could arrange for them to attend trial sessions at a sports club. Young people have a much broader range of activities available to them than many parents may have had growing up, so it can be worth exploring the scope of options available through local sports centres and organisations. This could even be a good opportunity for your teen to teach *you* a new activity, or for them to turn a session into a competition – old versus young!

Don't forget, if you are expecting your teen to be active it is only fair you provide them with appropriate shoes and equipment and that clean clothing is readily available on a daily basis. It can also be helpful to programme exercise in a diary

↑ Many gyms run teen-only gym sessions.

as it can be easy to change your mind if it is not a firm engagement, especially if taking place outside in poor weather.

Although the issue of weight is often an emotive subject, your teen may find it helpful as part of an exercise programme to keep a record of their body mass index (BMI) using a BMI calculator. Try using the NHS BMI calculator available online.

⬇ Your teen may find it helpful to be aware of their BMI.

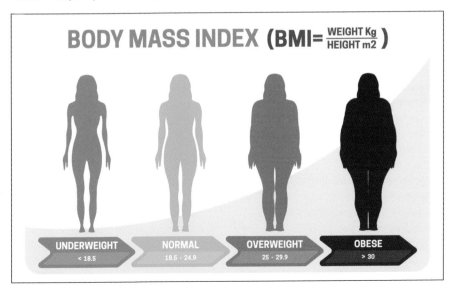

BODY MASS INDEX $\left(BMI = \frac{WEIGHT\ Kg}{HEIGHT\ m2}\right)$

UNDERWEIGHT	NORMAL	OVERWEIGHT	OBESE
< 18.5	18.5 - 24.9	25 - 29.9	> 30

Food and nutrition

A healthy diet should go hand in hand with an exercise programme. According to NHS guidance this should consist of:

- At least five portions of a variety of fruit and vegetables every day.
- Meals based around higher-fibre, starchy foods such as potatoes, bread, rice or pasta.
- Some dairy or dairy alternatives.
- Some beans, pulses, fish, eggs, meat and other protein.
- Unsaturated oils and spreads, in small amounts.
- At least six to eight glasses of fluids a day.
- Low fat, salt and sugar intake.

Vegetarianism and veganism

An increasing number of young people are choosing to adopt vegetarian, vegan or pescatarian diets. Vegetarians and vegans refrain from eating all meat, fish and animal by-products. Vegans also refrain from eating eggs or dairy products.

Pescatarians refrain from meat but do eat fish. It is difficult to place an accurate figure on the number of vegetarian and vegan young people in the UK; however, one poll conducted by the Linda McCartney food brand claims as many as 10% of young people aged 8–13 identify as vegetarian or vegan and 44% were choosing to lower their intake of meat and dairy products. Reasons given for changing diets included emulating people on social media, personal health and simply being interested in trying it out. An additional reason that has gained significant ground in recent years has been the purported negative impact of livestock on climate change.

According to NHS guidance there are no health concerns with your teen following a vegetarian or vegan diet as long as they receive the nutrients they need, including sufficient levels of iron, calcium, and vitamins B_{12} and D. Protein is also essential to a healthy diet, good sources of which include eggs, milk, cheese, soya, pulses, beans, nuts and seeds.

Eating disorders

It is thought that approximately 1.25 million people in the UK have a form of eating disorder, of whom 75% will be female. Common forms include:

- **Body dysmorphic disorder** (BDD or body dysmorphia) A common mental health condition affecting both males and females. Sufferers will be obsessed with perceived flaws in their appearance.
- **Bulimia** An eating disorder in which sufferers consume large amounts of food over a short period (binge eating) and then vomit or take laxatives to prevent weight gain.

⬇ Some 75% of people with eating disorders are female.

- **Anorexia** An eating disorder in which sufferers attempt to maintain a very low weight, often through undereating, exercise or a combination of both.

It is not always possible to tell if your teen has an eating disorder simply by looking at them. However, there are several signs that may trigger concern. These include your teen obsessing over their weight and shape, avoiding food and mealtimes, mood swings, lethargy, extremes in weight for their age and dizziness or nausea.

While eating disorders can be overcome, they can have long-lasting or permanent effects on the body and in extreme cases can prove fatal. Your teen's GP should be consulted, even if they refuse to attend with you. Local and national support groups are also available to provide regular advice and encouragement. It is important to consult official health sites offering professional guidance as a number of forums on the Internet actively seek to endorse unhealthy eating habits rather than offer solutions.

How to help your teen adopt a healthy attitude towards food

- Model good practice. If you are choosing unhealthy options and purchasing takeaways and junk food then don't expect your teen to make healthy choices.
- Ensure fruit and raw veg is available as a snack.
- Limit crisps, sweets, cakes and biscuits to treats, rather than as part of everyday consumption.
- Involve your teen in the family food shop. Try to plan a healthy shopping list and ensure you stick to it.
- Encourage your teen to look at food labelling to check levels of sugar, salt, fat (especially saturated fat) and calories. Be aware that nutritional labels often show quantities per 100g or per fraction of the packet, so actual levels may be a lot higher than initially thought.
- Discourage sugary drinks. Of particular concern should be the so-called 'energy' drinks – one popular brand contains a whopping 55g of sugar in a 500ml can!
- Download a calorie checker on your phones to check food information while shopping.
- Check if your teen's school provides a healthy and balanced food offer. Some schools are still selling energy drinks and fried food on a daily basis.
- Encourage your teen to cook with you or to cook a meal for the whole family. This can also double as a useful exercise in household budgeting.
- Do not stigmatise your teen if they have issues with their diet, and don't expect them to eat every type of food. There are probably some foods that would make *you* physically sick if you were forced to eat them.

⬇ Encourage your teen to read nutritional labels on food packaging.

Sleep

A healthy regime depends not just on activities and diet during the waking hours, but also on the amount, and quality, of sleep.

It may come as a surprise to learn that health professionals have found several serious health issues can be linked to a lack of quality sleep. These include heart disease, high blood pressure, diabetes, depression, anxiety and even weight gain.

The NHS recommends nine hours of sleep for an average teenager. This may prove difficult to achieve if your teen has to allocate a substantial part of their after-school hours to homework, clubs, music practice or part-time employment. However, there are still steps you can take to encourage your teen to get a good night's sleep:

■ Establish a regular bedtime. This may include staggered times for music/TV off and lights out.

■ Ensure your teen's bedroom is conducive to sleep. Is it clean, free of unpleasant smells and a comfortable temperature? Are curtains blocking any obtrusive light from outside?

■ Ensure electronic gadgets are turned off or removed from the bedroom. Social media updates will often be signalled by a distracting sound or flashing light when received and young people are usually tempted to check their social media accounts as soon as they receive a new text or update.

■ If your teen is listening to music or

⬇ The NHS recommends nine hours of sleep for an average teenager.

watching TV they should turn off equipment and remove any earphones before becoming overtired.

◼ Avoid consuming liquids close to sleep time, especially caffeine and energy drinks.

If your teen continues to suffer from poor sleep they should consult their GP as there may be an underlying medical issue.

⬇ Electronic gadgets should be turned off or removed from the bedroom.

Mental health

Another high-profile topic in the media is that of mental health – unfortunately not without justification. Across the age range 5–19, one in eight young people have been found to have at least one mental health disorder. Boys are more likely to suffer disorders at a younger age, while girls are more likely to suffer at an older age. Despite the high level of need, only one in four young people claiming a mental health disorder has sought help from a specialist service such as CAMHS.

CAMHS

Mental health services for young people in the UK are largely provided by the NHS under the heading CAMHS (Child and Adolescent Mental Health Services). The level of service may vary depending on location, but many teams consist of a range of professionals including psychiatrists, psychologists, social workers, nurses and substance misuse specialists. Young people and their parents can often self-refer to CAMHS, or a referral can be made by a GP, teacher, youth worker or other organisation on behalf of a young person. CAMHS referrals have continued to rise year on year, and as a result many authorities now have a waiting list.

⬇ Only one in four young people claiming a mental health disorder has sought help.

Mental health disorders

Mental health is a term that spans a vast number of conditions, far too many and complex to explore in this book, but which includes anxiety, depression, bipolar disorder, psychosis, schizophrenia and OCD (obsessive-compulsive disorder). Disorders can be caused by a chemical imbalance in the brain, but may also result from bullying, social media's portrayal of lifestyles and body images, gender issues or the consumption of drugs (both prescribed and illegal). While all disorders are serious concerns in themselves, they can also be a precursor to the horrific consequence of suicide or suicidal thoughts. In 2018 6,507 suicides were registered in the UK, three-quarters of which were among men. Although teen suicide rates are comparatively low, the rate among under-25s has increased in recent years, particularly among 10- to 24-year-old females.

⬇ Your teen may be too embarrassed to discuss their mental health with you.

How to support your teen

Your teen may be unwilling to share their feelings with you around issues of mental health, therefore it's important to be able to recognise some of the signs and symptoms of mental health disorders. These can include:

- Anxiety, depression, tearfulness and withdrawal from social situations.
- Changes in eating and sleeping habits, weight or appearance.
- Complaining of pains, headaches or lethargy.
- An obsession with death or dying, making Internet searches about suicide, giving away possessions or expressing remarks such as 'I wish I was dead', or 'no one will miss me'.

Although mental health issues should be taken very seriously, it's also important as a parent to realise signs and symptoms of mental health issues are surprisingly similar to the regular behaviour of many young people and are a common method of expressing teen frustration!

Regardless of your teen's intent, seek to reassure them and let them know you are taking their feelings seriously. Do not be tempted to belittle how they feel or say 'pull yourself together'.

Mental disorders are very real illnesses that can cripple a young person's ability to engage in all aspects of life. While some mental illnesses can be treated by talking methods such as CBT (cognitive behaviour therapy), others may need drugs to correct a chemical imbalance. It is worth noting that although some young people claim the use of cannabis can alleviate symptoms of mental health disorders, research has shown increased risks to mental health for regular users and young people whose brains are still developing.

To seek support, contact CAMHS or your teen's GP in the first instance. Your GP may be able to recommend specialist support groups for both your teen and the wider family, either locally or online. In instances where a life is at risk, always dial 999. If your teen is unwilling to engage with medical professionals they may still be prepared to speak with a teacher, youth worker or relative. Schools will also be able to access specialist provision such as counselling, educational psychologists and other professional support networks deemed appropriate. You can also point them in the direction of relevant literature or online resources from confidential support groups and medical professionals. The Samaritans offer 24/7 support to anyone struggling emotionally. They are contactable free of charge by calling 116 123 in the UK, and via email, post or in person. Full contact details can be found at Samaritans.org.

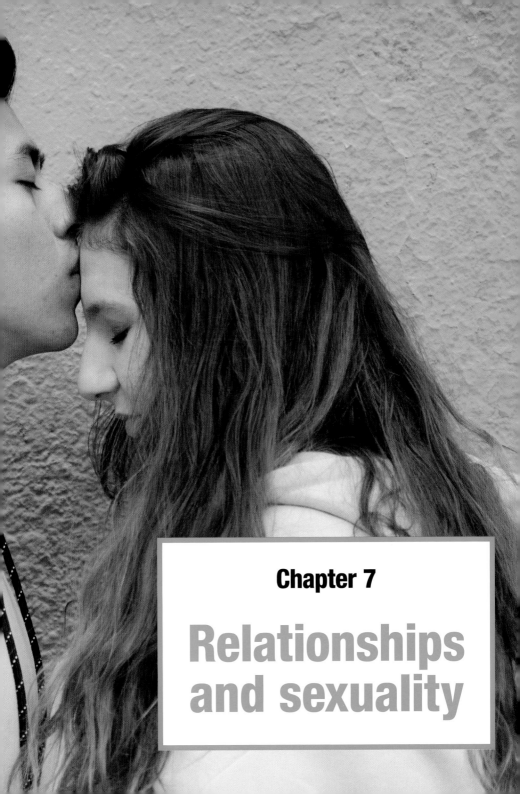

Chapter 7

Relationships
and sexuality

Sex and sexuality are probably the two topics that parents are least prepared to discuss with their teen. They are probably also the topics your teen is least willing to discuss with you! Thankfully, most primary and secondary schools include sex and relationship education as part of their curriculum.

What's more, despite the bad press around sex-related content online, the Internet hosts a wealth of professional, confidential and impartial information from organisations such as the NHS, available to your teen from the privacy of their own phone.

The teenage years are when most people develop not just stronger sexual urges, but a clearer awareness of their sexual identity. The debate around nature vs nurture determining sexual preference is still raging and is far too complex for this

⬇ The teenage years are when most young people develop their sexual identity.

book; however, the sexual identity of your teen is still an important issue for you as a parent – even if it's simply because it will be an important issue for them.

A 2017 ONS survey (published in 2019) found 93.2% of over-16s identified as heterosexual and 2% as lesbian, gay or bisexual (LGB). Males, people aged 16–24 and people living in London were more likely to identify as LGB. However, as the survey relates to a very personal issue it could be assumed that some responders may have been cautious in their responses.

Most parents of teens will have experienced their teenage years in a period

The rainbow flag is recognised worldwide as a symbol of the LGBTQ+ community.

when media portrayed non-heterosexual relationships as quirky, subversive, humorous or camp. This attitude has mellowed significantly through a mixture of initiatives including high-profile campaigning, broader education in schools, wider media coverage (especially via social media) and the implementation of laws covering behaviour in the workplace and wider society. That said, it is still possible that many parents feel in the dark or confused by the profusion of new terminology around sexual orientation that goes way beyond the basic definition of 'gay' and 'lesbian'.

Many members of the gay community identify under the banner of LGBTQ+ (lesbian, gay, bisexual, transgender, questioning and others). Questioning relates to persons still establishing their sexual identity. However, sexual and gender identity can now be defined employing a broader range of more specific terms, including:

- **Gender fluid** – a person who does not identify as a particular gender and may possibly move between genders.
- **Queer** – a person 'wanting to reject specific labels of romantic orientation, sexual orientation and/or gender identity'.
- **Trans** – trans people will identify as a different gender to that which was identified when they were born.

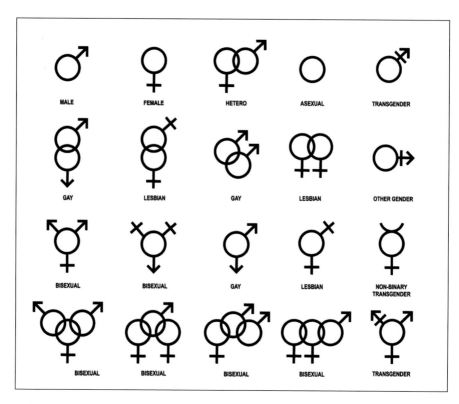

MALE	FEMALE	HETERO	ASEXUAL	TRANSGENDER
GAY	LESBIAN	GAY	LESBIAN	OTHER GENDER
BISEXUAL	BISEXUAL	GAY	LESBIAN	NON-BINARY TRANSGENDER
BISEXUAL	BISEXUAL	BISEXUAL	BISEXUAL	TRANSGENDER

⬆ Sexual and gender identity can now be defined employing a broader range of terms.

- **Cisgender** – cis means 'on the same side as', as opposed to 'trans' which means 'across', therefore cisgender people remain the gender they were identified as when born.
- **Pansexual/polysexual** – 'Someone who is pansexual is not limited in sexual choice based on biological sex, gender or gender identity.'
- **Intersex** – refers to 'a variety of conditions in which a person is born with a reproductive or sexual anatomy that doesn't seem to fit the typical definitions of female or male'.
- **Asexual** – a person not interested in sexual activity.

Despite significant advancements in education, tolerance and legislation, pockets of homophobia remain, and in some countries homosexual behaviour is still punishable by imprisonment and even death. It is therefore unsurprising that 'coming out' can be a traumatic experience, particularly for young people. For some young people coming out will seem impossible as it would mean being ostracised by family members or friends and acquaintances within a faith, social or work setting. Such trauma has been a significant factor in LGBTQ+ young people experiencing higher rates of depression, anxiety, bullying, self-harm and suicide.

It is vital that as parents we do all within our ability to provide a safe environment for our children, regardless of their gender.

Gender and sexuality are personal issues and you should never attempt to enforce your own personal choices or opinions on your teen. Be active in tackling incidents of homophobia when you encounter them. It may be safer for you to tackle an issue as a parent rather than your teen. However, you may wish to discuss this with them first, especially if approaching your teen's school. Most importantly, remember your teen is an individual. Don't assume stereotypes portrayed in the media apply to all individuals of a particular gender or sexuality.

If your teen is struggling with any aspect of their gender or sexuality, free, confidential and impartial advice and guidance can be found through various specialist organisations, some of which are listed in Chapter Nine.

Pressure to engage in sexual activity

Parents may have a concern around the notion their teen can have sex with whoever they wish and whenever they wish, thus possibly devaluing the concept of a long-term and committed relationship. Whatever your opinion as a parent, it is important to acknowledge that views around fidelity, marriage and the nature of sexual relationships are unique to each individual, and your teen's views may differ from yours. As hard as it may be for you to accept, this does not necessarily make them 'wrong'.

The average age for losing virginity in

⬇ The average age for losing virginity in the UK is thought to be between 16 and 17.

the UK is thought to be between 16 and 17. This is merely an average and age will vary greatly depending on several personal, religious, physical, mental or ethical factors. Your teen should never feel pressured by their peers, the media or other groups or individuals to engage in any sexual activity. However, if your teen is seeking to engage sexually they should carefully consider:

- Is their partner consenting?
- Have they discussed contraception? Do they have access to condoms to protect each other from STIs/STDs?
- Are both parties sober and not under the influence of any drugs?
- Do they love their partner? This is a very difficult issue for some couples who

⬇ Your teen should never feel pressured to engage in sexual activity.

may not be emotionally mature enough to understand the notion of 'love'. Other young people may consciously wish to partake in sex as an activity outside any confines of a romantic relationship, a concept some parents may find difficult to accept.

- Are they engaging in sex because they feel pressured, maybe because they fear losing their partner if they say no.
- Have they considered the impact of sex at a young age and outside a long-term relationship or marriage? Engaging in sex at an early age can lead to lifelong issues around regret and may compromise mental well-being.

Even if your teen has considered all these issues they are still bound by legislation in regard to sexual activity.

The law

The age of consent (the legal age to have any sexual activity) in the UK is 16. This applies to both males and females regardless of sexual orientation. It is an offence for anyone to have any sexual activity with a person under the age of 16 (or 18 if the older person is in a position of trust, such as a teacher). Although no one under the age of 16 can consent in law to sex, this does not mean the Crown Prosecution Service will seek legal action against two consenting teenagers of a similar age under the age of 16.

Teen pregnancy

One of the biggest fears for parents, particularly parents of daughters, is the risk of teen pregnancy. Although the stigma nowadays cannot be compared to that experienced even a few decades ago, the financial and social implications are still

depressingly negative. Teen pregnancy levels in parts of the UK are still higher than in many Western European countries and teenagers have a higher rate of unplanned pregnancy than other age groups. What's more, compared to older mothers, teenage mothers are more susceptible to stillbirths, low birth weight, infant mortality, developmental delays, income deprivation and the risk of becoming NEET (not in education, employment or training).

That said, despite regular scare stories in the media, the rate of teen pregnancy has actually fallen sharply and is now at the lowest level since 1969. This should come as no great surprise. Sex and relationship education in schools has become more robust, the Internet has opened up impartial, comprehensive and

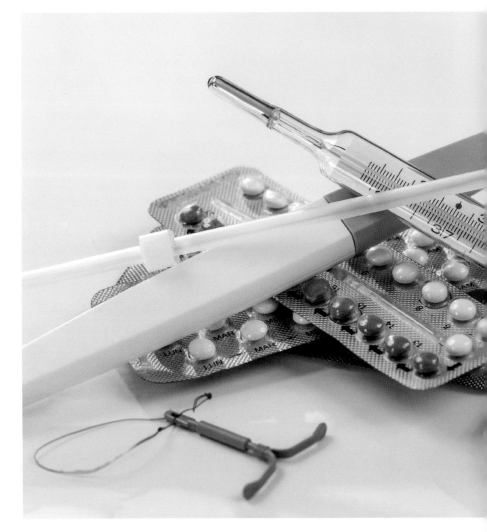

freely available advice and guidance with guaranteed anonymity, and academic and employment opportunities have increased significantly for young women. However, perhaps the most crucial factor has been the availability of the birth control pill and the ease and affordability of contraception.

⬇ The NHS currently offers 15 methods of contraception.

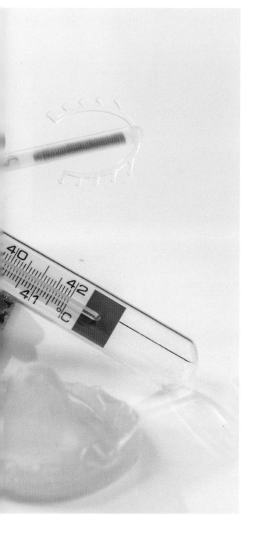

Contraception

The NHS currently offers 15 methods of contraception. Your teen should discuss the most appropriate method with their GP, who will take into consideration factors such as age, family history, smoking habits and medical history. Contraception is free on the NHS, including emergency contraception, also known as the morning after pill. Two forms of emergency contraception pill are available – Levonelle and ellaOne. Both can be obtained free of charge from:

- contraception clinics
- Brook centres
- some pharmacies
- most sexual health or genito-urinary medicine (GUM) clinics
- most NHS walk-in centres and minor injuries units
- most GP surgeries
- some hospital accident and emergency (A&E) departments.

Both forms can also be bought from most pharmacies, however you need to be 16 or over to purchase Levonelle.

ARE CONTRACEPTION ENQUIRIES CONFIDENTIAL OR WILL I BE INFORMED AS THE PARENT?
Contraception advice and prescribing is confidential. Parents will not be informed as long as your teen is not at risk of harm and is considered mature enough to understand the guidance and medication.

HOW EFFECTIVE IS CONTRACEPTION?
Your teen needs to understand that the only 100% safe form of birth control is abstinence. Otherwise, the most effective forms of contraception are currently the birth control implant and the IUD.

↑ Condoms are the only form of contraception that can protect against sexually transmitted infections.

CONDOMS

Although condoms are not 100% effective in preventing pregnancy, they are the only method of contraception that protects against passing on or receiving STIs/STDs. Free condoms are available to teenagers in most parts of the UK. The NHS website provides a searchable directory, detailing surgeries, pharmacies and other organisations supplying free condoms and support on contraception. Your teen should ensure any condoms they use carry the CE mark or BSI kite mark to ensure they meet rigorous quality assurance standards.

STDs/STIs, HIV and AIDS

Sexually transmitted infections (STIs, sometimes referred to as STDs), may not appear to have the same media presence as AIDS and HIV did in the 1980s and '90s, but all these issues are still very relevant in the 21st century. A Public Health England study found in 2018 there were 447,694 cases of sexually transmitted infections in England, a 5% increase since 2017. This included a rise in both chlamydia and gonorrhoea over the previous year.

In addition to the use of condoms, Public Health England recommends

sexually active teens should be screened annually for chlamydia, and 'on change of sexual partner', and receive annual HIV testing if your teen is having 'condomless sex with new or casual partners'. In addition, 'Gay, bisexual and other men who have sex with men should test annually for HIV and STIs and every three months if having condomless sex with new or casual partners.' Chlamydia test kits are available free of charge from most GP surgeries, pharmacies, health centres and youth centres.

My daughter is pregnant!

Pregnancy is a highly emotive subject for all concerned, whether it is a welcome state or otherwise. Although parents will be keen to share their views on a pregnancy, they should be wary of enforcing opinions and should ensure impartial advice and guidance is sought via a GP who will be able to refer your daughter to counselling and advice services. The three main options available to your daughter will be:

- Carrying the child to term and keeping the baby
- Carrying the child to term and giving the baby up for adoption
- Having an abortion.

A number of support agencies for expectant or young parents are listed in Chapter Nine of this book.

Chapter 8

Post-16 options

Given the relentless role of being a parent, it can be easy to forget that the teenage years will eventually draw to a close and your son or daughter will be setting foot into the world of work or further education.

Once statutory education ends your teen will have a number of options available. However, access to these will often depend on the level of their GCSE results. Since 2019 GCSEs (level 2 qualifications) have been graded from level 9 to level 1, with 1 being the lowest grade (apart from U for ungraded), and 4 considered a standard pass. Some schools may make reference to a baccalaureate. The EBacc (English Baccalaureate) measures attainment across a group of GCSEs including English, maths, science, languages, history and geography.

Old grades	New grades
A* A	9 8 7
B C	6 5 (strong pass) 4 (standard pass)
D E F G	3 2 1
U	U

Level 3 courses

Entry to level 3 courses, consisting mostly of A levels or BTEC level 3s, usually requires four or five GCSE passes at level 4 or above including English and maths (and occasionally science), although it is possible on some level 3 courses to retake English and maths. Requirements vary depending on the course and the institution, so it is vital you and your teen

research all options thoroughly before making any applications.

Many schools will have sixth forms (sometimes referred to as upper schools), that offer year 12 and 13 tuition in three or four subjects chosen by your teen. Sixth forms may also offer a range of BTEC courses. It is important to note that some BTECs offered at sixth form will not allow your teen to gain the same number of

credits or points for university as a full-time BTEC at college as they are studied for fewer hours and are often combined with A levels.

A college of further education (FE) will often offer BTEC courses but some may also offer A level tuition. Both A levels and BTEC Level 3s are acceptable for entry into higher education (HE), which typically refers to university-level study. Universities provide

⬆ Passes at A level or BTEC Level 3 can allow your teen to access university study.

a range of courses between level 4 and level 8, with most students studying a BA or BSc degree. Each university sets its own entry requirements. These can be viewed by visiting the university's own website or via the UCAS (University and Colleges Admissions Service) website at ucas.com.

Tuition fees by region for courses starting in 2020				
Student's home region	Studying in England	Studying in Scotland	Studing in Wales	Studying in Northern Ireland
England	Up to £9,250	Up to £9,250	Up to £9,250	Up to £9,250
Scotland	Up to £9,250	No fee	Up to £9,250	Up to £9,250
Wales	Up to £9,250	Up to £9,250	Up to £9,000	Up to £9,250
Northern Ireland	Up to £9,250	Up to £9,250	Up to £9,250	Up to £4,395
EU	Up to £9,250	No fee	Up to £9,250	Up to £4,395
Other international	Variable	Variable	Variable	Variable

Funding for FE and HE courses

Foundation courses in reading, writing and basic maths are free. Under 24-year-olds studying for their first qualification to GCSE, A level or equivalent standard can also often access free education. Your teen should consult with their local college or careers adviser for details pertaining to a particular school or college.

Universities are currently capped as to the amount they can charge students per year. These figures, shown in the table above from UCAS, depend upon the region of the UK and the student's home region.

Student loans are available to cover HE fees, and are repayable, with interest, once your teen earns a level of income designated by the government. Current levels can be found at gov.uk.

Alternatives to sixth form and FE

Although most young people will enter sixth form or college on leaving year 11, these are not the only routes available. Apprenticeships have become increasingly popular, offering academic qualifications alongside paid employment. They take between one and five years to complete and can allow study up to HE level.

Full-time employment is another possible option for your teen. However, in England a young person under the age of 18 must also receive a minimum of 280 hours per year of part-time education or training.

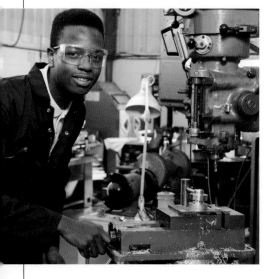

← An apprenticeship will allow your teen to earn money while gaining a qualification.

For young people not yet ready to access the above options, several short-term schemes are run around the UK, often by charitable organisations such as The Prince's Trust. These generally last from ten weeks to a year and allow your teen to enhance their social, academic and personal skills before progressing into work or FE study.

Education and careers advice

Although it is useful for your teen to discuss education and career routes with parents, friends and relatives, it is essential they also seek impartial information, advice and guidance from a professional careers adviser. Most parents will have received guidance during their final year of formal education via a representative of the Careers Service. The Careers Service morphed into Connexions in 2000 and was disbanded in 2012 to be replaced with the National Careers Service (contactable via phone and online). Your teen should also have access via their school or college to an impartial careers adviser (from years 8–13) in addition to a careers tutor. However, parents should note that as careers advisers are now employed directly by schools there is some debate nationally as to the level of impartiality young people can expect to receive.

Chapter 9

Where to go for help

If you've made it this far through the book you are possibly wondering how you can ever be expected to offer the required level of support for your teen. The good news is that your job is to be the parent, offering love and security, and while it is sensible to be armed with as much knowledge as possible, there are a number of organisations a click or phone call away that can offer free, professional and confidential support and guidance. In fact, the scope of organisations supporting young people is far too wide to provide a comprehensive directory here, but below you can find a select list of some of the agencies currently active within the UK.

Careers and education

National Careers Service
Government-established careers service for young people.
nationalcareers.service.gov.uk
0800 100 900 plus webchat.

Job Centre Plus
Search portal and support for employment vacancies.
www.gov.uk/contact-jobcentre-plus

Apprenticeships
Search portal and support network for apprenticeship vacancies throughout the UK.

England: National Apprenticeship Service
nationalhelpdesk@findapprenticeship.
    service.gov.uk
    Telephone: 0800 015 0400
Scotland: www.apprenticeships.scot
Northern Ireland: www.nidirect.gov.uk
Wales: ams.careerswales.com

UCAS
Universities and Colleges Admission Service for information on all HE courses.
www.ucas.com

Carers

Young Carers
Support for young carers (someone under 18 who helps look after someone in their family, or a friend, who is ill, disabled or misuses drugs or alcohol).
carers.org

Barnardos
Support covering a wide range of issues relating to young people and families.
www.barnardos.org.uk

Young Scot
Information and advice for young people in Scotland including young carers.
young.scot

NHS
Comprehensive health and well-being site including information around caring.
www.nhs.uk

Child protection/safeguarding
It is everybody's duty to protect young people. If you are aware of a young person at risk of harm you should contact the police on 101 (or 999 if they are in immediate danger). You can also notify the safeguarding team at your local authority.

National Domestic Abuse Helpline
Support for family members experiencing domestic abuse.
www.nationaldahelpline.org.uk
0808 2000 247

The Hideout
Support around domestic violence.
thehideout.org.uk

Relate
Relationship support.
www.relate.org.uk
0300 003 0396 or via webchat.

NSPCC
National organisation targeting child abuse.
www.nspcc.org.uk

Childline
Free 24/7 confidential helpline for children.
www.childline.org.uk
0800 1111

Bullying UK
Advice and guidance for parents and young people around the issue of bullying.
www.bullying.co.uk
0808 800 2222

Kidscape
Support around issues of bullying and sexual abuse.
info@kidscape.org.uk
0845 1205 204
0207 7303300

SupportLine
Confidential emotional support.
www.supportline.org.uk
01708 765200
info@supportline.org.uk

Counselling and support

School/college counselling services
All schools, colleges and HE institutions will have designated counselling support. Contact your institution's student support officer.

Local authority
Many local authorities will provide their own counselling and support services. Contact your local county or unitary authority.

CAMHS
Mental health support for young people. Access via your GP or directly by searching for a local support provider via www.nhs.uk.

Samaritans
Charity dedicated to reducing feelings of isolation and disconnection that can lead to suicide.
www.samaritans.org
116 123

Brook
Pregnancy support.
www.brook.org.uk

Family Lives
Support for young parents.
www.familylives.org.uk

The Mix
Free confidential help and support for under 25-year-olds.
0808 808 4994 (1–11pm every day) or email via online form at
www.themix.org.uk.

Kooth
Free, safe and anonymous online support for young people.
www.kooth.com

Cruse Bereavement Care
Provides information on what you can do to help a child or young person who is grieving.
www.cruse.org.uk
0844 477 9400

The Hideout
Support around domestic violence.
thehideout.org.uk

Relate
Relationship support.
www.relate.org.uk
0300 003 0396 or via webchat.

NSPCC
National organisation targeting child abuse.
www.nspcc.org.uk

Childline
Free 24/7 confidential helpline for children.
www.childline.org.uk
0800 1111

Bullying UK
Advice and guidance around the issue of bullying for parents and young people.
www.bullying.co.uk
0808 800 2222

Kidscape
Support around issues of bullying and sexual abuse.
info@kidscape.org.uk
0845 1205 204
0207 730 3300

SupportLine
Confidential emotional support.
www.supportline.org.uk
01708 765200
info@supportline.org.uk

Big Deal
Support around gambling and gambling addiction.
www.bigdeal.org.uk

There are numerous counsellors and psychotherapists providing private counselling. Sessions will incur a consultation fee (often £40+ per hour). Professional counsellors and therapists can be sought by contacting the **British Association for Counselling and Psychotherapy (BACP)** via www.bacp.co.uk or by calling 0870 443 5252.

Drugs, alcohol and smoking
FRANK
Comprehensive information base around the issue of drugs.
www.talktofrank.com

Turning Point
Support around drugs, alcohol, mental health and learning disabilities.
turning-point.co.uk

NHS Smokefree
Stop smoking service.
0300 123 1044

Alcoholics Anonymous
Support around issues with alcohol and alcoholism.
www.alcoholics-anonymous.org.uk
0800 9177 650
help@aamail.org

Gangs and crime
Victim Support
Victim Support helps people cope with the effects of crime.
www.victimsupport.org.uk
0845 30 30 900

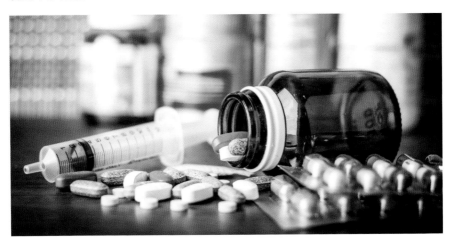

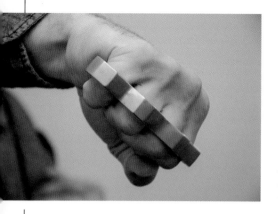

Rape Crisis (England and Wales)
Support for victims of rape or sexual violence. 0808 802 9999 (12–2.30pm and 7–9.30pm every day of the year) or online chat via rapecrisis.org.uk.

Health (inc. mental and sexual health)

NHS
All health-related issues including eating disorders, mental health and sexual health. www.nhs.uk

Crimestoppers
Crimestoppers is an independent UK-wide charity working to stop crime. You can call them anonymously.
www.crimestoppers-uk.org
0800 555 111

CAMHS
Mental health support for young people. Access via your GP or directly by searching for a local support provider via www.nhs.uk.

Suzy Lamplugh Trust
Offers confidential advice to children and adults to help them stay safe and recognise potentially dangerous situations.
www.suzylamplugh.org

Samaritans
Charity dedicated to reducing feelings of isolation and disconnection that can lead to suicide.
www.samaritans.org
116 123

Brook
Pregnancy support.
www.brook.org.uk

Family Lives
Support for young parents.
www.familylives.org.uk

MIND
Mental health support.
0300 123 3393
info@mind.org.uk
Text: 86463

Young Minds
Young people's mental health support.
0808 802 5544 or via online form at
youngminds.org.uk.

Tommy's
*Support with issues relating to pregnancy,
childbirth and stillbirth.*
www.tommys.org

Sexwise
*All aspects of sexual well-being including
contraception, safe sex and pregnancy.*
www.sexwise.fpa.org.uk

Housing
Most housing enquiries (other than those
relating to private rental agreements)
should be discussed with your local
authority in the first instance. Local
authorities will have a designated under-
18s housing adviser.

Shelter
Housing and homelessness support.
www.shelter.org.uk
0808 800 4444

Centrepoint
*Housing and homelessness support for
young people aged 16–25.*
centrepoint.org.uk
0808 800 0661 or via webchat.

Foyer
*Housing and homelessness support for
young people aged 16–25.*
foyer.net
0207 430 2212
inbox@foyer.net

LGBTQ+
Young Stonewall
*Support for the young LGBTQ+
community.*
www.youngstonewall.org.uk
Freephone 0800 0502020

FFLAG (Families and Friends of
Lesbians and Gays)
*Support for the young LGBTQ+
community.*
www.fflag.org.uk

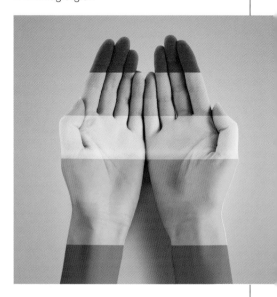

Index